CARBON UNDER PRESSURE

Meg Heart

A catalogue record for this work is available from the National Library of Australia

NATIONAL LIBRARY OF AUSTRALIA

National Library of Australia Catalogue-in-Publication data:
Carbon Under Pressure/Meg Heart

ISBN: 978-0-6452558-1-2 (Paperback)
ISBN: 978-0-6452558-2-9 (Ebook)

Disclaimer:

Events described in these pages are based on real events, reasonable opinion and honest belief of real-world situations. The names of all people who appear in this book have been changed, with the exception of Jeff Kennett who agreed to appear as himself in these pages. Any resemblance to persons living or dead resulting from changes to names or identifying details is entirely coincidental and unintentional. The names of all locations have been changed or omitted.

Content Guidance:

This book refers to self-harm, attempted suicide, sexual abuse, emotional abuse, domestic abuse, childhood trauma, mental health, anxiety and depression. There are raw descriptions of emotional scenes, and minor swearing in context. See more content guidance at www.megheart.com

This book is dedicated to everyone who soldiers on in silence. May you find your voice to heal, and share your story to heal others.

Foreword

When I first met Rose, I was captivated by her radiance. I expected her face to show traces of the suffering that must have tormented her for years, but what I saw before me was a woman with a broad, sunny smile and warm, sincere eyes.

She was passionate about writing this book, and she wanted me to help her. It's not always easy for people to find the right words to express their experiences in writing. They've felt the emotions, but rarely spoken about them. They've carried their secrets in silence for so long, words can be hard to find.

Rose told me her story with brutal honesty. She held nothing back, and I immediately knew this story was powerful. I began to see her life as if in a movie, and the words flowed easily onto the page. This harsh and haunting story wants to be told. It beckons you urgently inside Rose's life and tugs you towards raw moments that will make you gasp. It's rare to find someone as honest as Rose, which makes sharing her story even more important.

But Rose has been doubly silenced. To publish this book under her own name, Rose would have been required, for legal reasons, to exclude some events from these pages. Removing those scenes never crossed her mind. For Rose, telling the full story is more important than the telling of her name.

And so, in a strange twist, it is the author rather than the ghostwriter of *Carbon Under Pressure* who remains anonymous. But she does not remain unknown. As you read this book you will learn things about

Rose that even some of her closest friends didn't know. Her willingness to expose her most challenging moments is driven by a desire to inspire change, and she is content to let these pages speak for themselves.

Writing with Rose was an honor.

– Martina Sheehan
Ghostwriter

Contents

Introduction

I wish we lived in a world where what you are about to read could never happen, but we don't. This is the story of Rose, an ordinary woman facing extraordinary circumstances. Events like this are happening right now, maybe to someone you know, or maybe even to you. What happened to Rose could happen to anyone.

If you recognise your journey in these pages, rest assured you are not alone. Speak out; reach out. There are people who care. For others, this story will open your eyes to the fragility of those who soldier on in resigned silence when their world has been shattered. I hope you will listen deeply when they break their silence, and add your voice to theirs when they speak up for change. Together we can create a more compassionate, respectful and honourable society.

– Meg Heart

Chapter 1
Waking Up

Sunday, 11:45pm

The gentle breath on my face and soft muffled whispers were surely a dream. But I sensed a presence beside my bed, and as I stirred, the whispers took form. They were words I will never forget: "Mum, I'm so sorry, I can't do this anymore. Please forgive me."

All parents know the sudden wakefulness that strikes when one of their children is suffering. From the moment we hear their first newborn cry we are attuned to their needs, and even at sixteen, Sophie's words shook me from my sleep.

"What's the matter?" I asked as the faint shape of my daughter came into focus.

"It's okay Mum, go back to sleep."

I sensed a heavy sadness in her voice and realised my face was wet from her tears. As she backed away, my eyes adjusted to the hazy light cast by a waning moon and I noticed there was a large dark patch on the front of her white pyjama shirt. A disturbing unease swept over me. Something was terribly wrong.

Then, like a phantom receding into the night, she turned and walked out the door.

I crept quickly out of bed, careful not to wake Stuart, and followed her to the lounge room. That's where I found her, slumped on the couch.

The dark patch on her shirt was blood. Shock struck me like a hammer blow to the chest. I rushed to her side and lifted her shirt. Raw, deep slashes marbled her abdomen and the tops of her legs. She tried weakly to push me away, then I noticed the blood smeared on her hands and arms and across the couch where she lay.

"What happened? What have you done?" I cried. My voice fired questions before my eyes could comprehend what I was seeing.

"I can't do this anymore," she responded groggily.

"Have you taken something?" I looked up at her face, my eyes probing for some clue, some answer to make sense of the scene before me.

There was no response.

"Sophie tell me ... what have you done?"

Her eyes were closed and her skin was pale, her body now completely limp.

Frantic, I ran to the kitchen for the first aid kit, the instinctive response of a mother confronted with her child's injuries. There on the bench was an empty packet of sleeping pills. *Oh no. She's trying to kill herself!*

I ran back to the lounge room and collapsed at Sophie's side, trying once more to stir her. "How many pills have you taken?" My quivering hands tried to find some sign of life, but she still didn't move.

Then I screamed.

⌣

Before that fateful night, I thought my life was complete. I'd left an unhappy marriage and been rewarded with new love. I'd shrugged off the judgement and disapproval of my family to forge life on my own terms. I'd changed jobs and moved cities. I thought I'd learnt a lot about myself. I thought I'd been brave. I thought the worst was behind me, but nothing could prepare me for what was to come.

⌒

"Stuart. Stuart!" I cried out for my husband. "Wake up. Help. She's tried to overdose!"

I continued shaking Sophie, willing her to respond. "Come on baby, wake up. Come on." Stuart stumbled into the room and was quickly at my side. "What's going on?" My words tumbled over each other; "She's taken sleeping pills. I don't know how many. She won't wake up!"

I backed away as Stuart checked over Sophie's limp body. Standing at the end of the couch with my hands clenched tightly at my face, I rocked back and forth, quietly repeating the words, "Come on baby ..." Fear immobilised me. I was petrified, powerless, watching the scene as if from another dimension.

"Call an ambulance, Rose." Stuart's urgent voice shook me from my stupor and back into action. I ran in frenzied circles, brushing up hard against a wall and sweeping aside items on the table in a desperate search for my phone. The whole house felt unfamiliar. I couldn't think. I was focused solely on hunting for the phone, a lifeline to save my daughter.

With violently shaking hands I dialled the emergency number and watched Stuart scoop Sophie up. Her tiny figure almost disappeared in his arms, and he carried her to the bathroom. As I followed him in, my call was answered. "I need an ambulance. My daughter is unconscious. We need help!"

Stuart held Sophie's face over the toilet, trying to put his fingers down her throat in an attempt to make her vomit. She was weakly turning her head away and murmuring, "Just let me be, please let me be." With some relief at these signs of life, I was able to start answering the operator's questions.

"How many pills has she taken?"

"I don't know. The packet is empty, but I don't know how many there were. They were prescribed to me six years ago. I think I took a few of them, but I can't be certain."

Realising his attempts were futile, Stuart picked Sophie up and took her back to the lounge room to wait for the ambulance.

I followed, still responding to the operator's questions. "Yes, she's very drowsy."

"Can you please say 'now' every time she breathes."

"Now."

A few seconds passed.

"Now."

Another few seconds.

"Now."

Once the operator decided Sophie's breathing was stable, she continued with her questions. I confirmed our address and our names, and felt a short moment of relief to know help was on its way.

All the while, Stuart was sitting beside Sophie tenderly stroking her cheek, brushing wisps of her long blonde hair back from her face and talking to her in a calm voice. Her eyes were closed but she was no longer limp and lifeless. Clinging tightly to my phone, I paced in a circle from the lounge room into the hallway, out the front door and back again. Surging waves of terror rushed through my body; "Is she getting any worse? How did this happen? Why did she do it?"

"Rose. Stop." Stuart's voice was firm as he turned to look up at me. "You are making the situation worse. Deep breaths, go to the front door and wait for the ambulance."

Reaching the door, I directed all my agitation down the line to the operator. "How far away are they? Why is it taking so long?" She reassured me the ambulance was nearly there.

Now pacing from the front door out to the street, I peered desperately into the gloom. The moon cast a distorted spotlight on our suburban drama, and as if on cue, the silence was broken by the faint sound of an approaching siren. When it turned into our street, the siren went quiet and the flashing red and blue lights transformed the dim gardens into a ghostly backdrop, lending an even more sinister air to our unfolding nightmare.

The next few minutes were a blur. The paramedics were calm, but they worked fast. As they leaned over to assess Sophie, I returned to the kitchen for the empty packet of pills. When I returned they had already placed an intravenous line in her arm and were transferring her to a stretcher. After loading Sophie into the back of the ambulance, the driver invited me into the front seat to travel with them. My heart was racing but my mind was blank. At that moment I was only capable of following the directions of others, and it didn't occur to me to change out of my pyjamas or take anything other than the phone, which I still held tightly in my hand. I just needed to be with my daughter.

All the way to the hospital I kept repeating, "I don't know how this happened. How could it happen?" The paramedic was kind and reassuring, seemingly all too accustomed to this dreadful scene. When we pulled into the emergency bay at the hospital, Sophie was rushed straight in, and one of the paramedics ushered me to the reception area, telling me to take a seat until I was called.

Finally alone, I felt tears prick my eyes. Shock was retreating, but the numbness was replaced by an excruciating pain. *What happened to my innocent girl? What was so dreadful to make her do this? Did I do something wrong? Was there something going on that I hadn't noticed?* The questions raced through my mind and I felt faint. Suddenly Stuart appeared at my side, and I melted into his arms.

The nightmare I woke to that evening blindsided me. Nightmares are supposed to happen as we sleep; we should be able to wake up and shake them off, but instead it was in waking that I came upon a secret inside my life I had missed. It had been draining my daughter of her innocence and her will to live for longer than I could imagine. It took me a long time to find out why.

Chapter 2
The Phone Call

I lifted my head from Stuart's shoulder when I heard my name being called. The doctor advised us they were treating Sophie for a drug overdose, but she would be okay and we could see her soon. He continued, "It was a suicide attempt and we've also found scars from previous episodes of self-harm. She will need a full psychiatric assessment. We're admitting her to the children's mental health ward."

With those words I was thrust into a world I had never envisaged. In my version of 'a parent's worst nightmare', I'd fretted over everything from stranger danger to car accidents and underage drinking, but I was unprepared for *this*. I had no experience with the sort of danger that would compel my daughter to attempt to take her own life. I wasn't oblivious to teenage mental health problems, but I never thought it would happen to us.

I was a fairly protective mother when my children were young, and I would veto their plans if they wanted to do something I thought was inappropriate for their age. However, I was also mindful of not holding them back. I always trusted them, but I knew how easily they could find themselves in a situation they couldn't handle. I'd done my fair share of sneaking out at night, trying to escape my controlling mother when I was a teenager, and I knew the dangers. When I was sixteen, I climbed out my bedroom window and joined my friends on an expedition to the city's nightclub precinct. We wanted to dance and drink and thought we were safe, but some time during the night I went into the nightclub's bathroom and an older man followed me in. He pushed me against the wall and started assaulting me. I was terrified, frozen with fear and unable to fight him off. Thankfully another girl walked in and the man ran out, but my saviour was so drunk she didn't even notice what was happening. When my friends found me, I was still shaking.

The experience made me very conscious of warning my children about the risks outside the safety of our home; about the dangers lying 'out there'. I convinced myself I was protecting them, but I never considered for one moment I would need to protect them from themselves. How do you stop your child from harming herself? How do you keep her safe from threats lurking in the secluded spaces of her own mind? I had no idea how to fix this. How could I protect Sophie from something I couldn't see or understand?

⌒

Stuart interrupted my spiralling thoughts by gently slipping a plastic cup of warm coffee into my hands. "Let's wait and see what comes next, Rose. We'll find out more soon." I was grateful for the steadfast love of this man. The last three years of my life with him by my side had renewed my faith in the power of love. The ease with which we met and fell in love was genuinely unexpected. It followed years of turmoil, which had shattered my family and left me full of self-doubt. A friend's suggestion to register with an online dating app seemed more of a distraction than a plan. When Stuart and I both swiped right, for me it was all about his eyes. There was something open and sincere about them, even in a photo, but it was still several weeks before we met. First we sent messages, then talked on the phone before graduating to video calls. I wanted to know more, hear more, sense more about him before I was prepared to even consider risking my heart. One thing I know about myself is that when I love, I love unconditionally, so if I was going to let someone in, I had to be sure. After spending more than twenty years with a man whose charisma proved to be a shallow disguise, my radar was heightened. I'd begun to trust my intuition, something that had never been encouraged by my parents and was even more harshly ridiculed within my first marriage. I was determined not to subject myself to another person who would tear me down, neither friend nor lover.

As I took a few sips of the coffee, Stuart gently suggested it might be time to call Sophie's father.

～

We rarely spoke. Discovering his affair early in our marriage was merely the first in a series of revelations about his duplicitous life that left me tormented by disbelief and outrage. It would take me a further ten years and more crushing revelations to find the courage to end the relationship once and for all, and when we eventually separated, Sophie was only thirteen years old.

Despite our differences, the most important thing was the wellbeing of our children. For Sophie's sake it was important for us to rally around. Surely he would feel the same and fly in to be by his daughter's side.

It was 3am when I walked outside into the chill night air and apprehensively pressed his number on my phone.

I heard the click as the phone was answered. "It's Rose. Sophie is in hospital."

"What happened?" he asked.

"She attempted suicide. She found some old sleeping tablets."

"How much did she take?"

"I don't know. I only took a few when the doctor gave them to me and I don't know how many were left. She also cut herself badly. The doctors are treating her. They said she will be okay, but she needs a full psychiatric assessment."

His tone changed abruptly. "You and Sophie are just attention seeking. You need to stop making this out to be bigger than it is," he barked down the phone.

His condescending and critical voice sent a chill right through me. I should have been prepared for it, but I wasn't. An old familiar dread stirred deep in my gut. *Oh shit, he is going to say I caused this or accuse me of not being a fit mother, like he did when I finally worked up the courage to leave him.*

"Rose, she is not suicidal. Let's face it, if someone really wants to kill themselves, they will just do it. She needs to toughen up and get over it."

My cold body was suddenly flooded with red-hot anger. "I can't believe what I am hearing! Our daughter is sick and needs our help. Whatever *you* think, something is seriously wrong. We're lucky we were there in time. Surely you can see that? You need to get down here so she has both of us supporting her." I was holding the phone in front of my face, directing all my rage through the invisible airwaves. But when my tirade ended, I touched the screen and saw the line was dead. He was gone.

I shouldn't have been surprised at his behaviour. It was his modus operandi to twist a situation around, trying to convince me I was wrong, trying to take control and rob me of my opinions and ideas. But how could he be so callous about Sophie? How could he brush off such a desperate act with 'get over it'?

I raised my face to the dark sky, grateful I'd at least had the foresight to make the call outside in the carpark. Willing the icy air to clear the oppressive veil of hostility and loathing that prickled my skin, I took a moment to breathe deeply. When I returned back through the hospital entrance, I found Stuart waiting inside. I told him what happened and he wrapped his reassuring arms around me. "We are here for her. We will do whatever it takes to support Sophie and get her the help she needs."

It was some time before we were guided into a room to see Sophie. She was sleeping, and it gave me some comfort to rest my face for a moment against her warm skin. My daughter was still alive, and that meant there was hope. The nurse told us she would be transferred to the ward when she woke, and we should come back later in the day when more would be known.

~

The clock struck 7am as Stuart and I walked through our front door. We were both exhausted and had shared few words on the drive home. The house was just the way we left it, with discarded wrappings from the paramedics' medical items and blood-stained towels from our bathroom strewn across the floor. When I noticed the blood on the couch and the carpet, I rushed into the kitchen and grabbed a cloth and a bottle of soda water from the fridge. Crouching down beside the couch, I poured soda water over the blood stains and scrubbed hard. Stuart knelt silently beside me with another cloth and did the same. I could feel his eyes watching me, assessing my furious strokes. Perhaps he was concerned I'd reached my breaking point, but I was determined not to lose control. I needed to remove the blood before it left a permanent mark. I wanted to wipe away all traces of the night. I wished I could erase the whole ordeal and find a way to forget this nightmare had ever happened.

I knew there was no way I could go to work. Nervously, I called my boss, unsure exactly what to say. In the end I simply told her the truth and she was amazing. She confided in me that her son suffered depression a number of years earlier, and at one stage had also been suicidal. She suggested I find a good psychologist who could give Sophie the tools to help her get through life. I asked her so many questions, my mind hungry for answers. I was good at plans and I knew how to work hard. If I could just find the right steps to get Sophie through this, I felt confident I could solve it. As I hung up the phone I felt a new sense of urgency. *That's what I'll do. I'll find a great psychologist and we'll do whatever needs to be done.* I couldn't sleep or stop to make myself a decent breakfast. Once my mind grabbed hold of a solution, it shifted into overdrive. When something is broken you dig deep and fix it, right?

Chapter 3
Rejection

I retraced my path to the hospital. Although I'd left only two hours earlier, the building felt unfamiliar. Now there were staff, patients and visitors wandering in all directions. I followed signs to elevators and down corridors until I found the entrance to the hospital's mental health ward. Harsh overhead lights lent a cold and clinical glare to the long corridor. The click of my heels echoed off the hard walls, and I saw there were cameras positioned on every corner. The receptionist confirmed Sophie had been admitted earlier, then asked me for some form of identification. I handed over my driver's licence, and as she disappeared into another room, I noticed all the doors were swipe locked and security staff were walking the floor. A few minutes later, the receptionist ushered me into a room and asked me to wait.

I tried to imagine where Sophie was behind all those locked doors. I wondered if she was terrified, waking up in a strange and sterile hospital room. *What were they doing with her? What did a psychiatric assessment involve?* I yearned to hold my child in my arms, to feel her soft golden hair and inhale the smell of her pure peachy skin. I desperately wanted to reassure her she was not alone.

I'd never faced a hospital visit like this before, where I could not see my sick child immediately. My children had been in hospital for various reasons during their childhood: inflamed tonsils, broken arms, ear infections. In my experience, children's wards are usually fairly cheerful places with lots of colour and warmth, but this place was hauntingly quiet and devoid of any positive energy. I felt out of my depth, unsure what to expect. I'd arrived confident we could find a solution, but with every passing moment the isolation allowed me too much time to think and my confidence plummeted. Unanswered questions once again invaded my mind: *Why did she do this? What happened? How would I get her through this?*

Another woman finally arrived and sat across the table from me. I can't recall if she explained her role, but she had a kindly face and steady eyes, and as she put her clipboard down on the table she assured me Sophie was safe. They were assessing her, she explained, and it would take some time. When I asked if I could see her, she promised she would bring her out shortly. First she wanted to ask me some questions.

"How has her mental state been lately?"

"What is her relationship like with her father?"

"Is she doing well at school? Does she have friends?"

"Does she have social media? Are there any issues there?"

Even though I'd been asking myself an endless stream of questions over the last few hours, I hadn't come up with any satisfactory answers. During the previous week, Sophie had seemed happier than ever, chatting about the new school year and helping me around the house more than usual. But that night she skipped dinner and went to bed early. I found out later she thought it would be more effective to take the tablets on an empty stomach. Discovering she was planning the attempt on her own life while we were all laughing and enjoying ourselves was a real wake-up call. I felt so guilty. I should have seen the signs. How could I have been unaware something was so wrong?

Answering the woman's questions was difficult. It forced me to talk about a past I rarely revealed. "My divorce from her father was nasty and emotional. It was almost four years ago," I explained.

～

As the youngest, I knew it had been an especially difficult time for Sophie. She was only ten years old when I first realised my marriage was beyond repair, but the thought of turning my children's lives upside down seemed cruel. I convinced myself I should wait until Sophie finished school, which left me facing another seven years living in the same house with a man whose cruel behaviour undermined my confidence and made me feel worthless.

In the end we never made it that far. When Sophie was thirteen, the marriage became untenable. Our separation was more like a stand-off; we continued to reside in the same home for almost one year, avoiding each other as much as possible. By the time we divorced, the situation was bitter and distressing. The very thing I dreaded – turning my children's lives upside down – seemed unavoidable. As the one who had initiated the break-up, my guilt intensified when I sold our long-time family home, various pieces of furniture that held memories of happier times, and even Sophie's treasured horse. Blinded by remorse, I felt compelled to give him everything, and I walked away with very little.

I struggled terribly during that period, feeling sad and lost. It was a dismal environment for my children, and just months after her father moved out, Sophie moved in with him. His work kept him away from home many nights of the week, and the attraction of freedom and minimal parental control for a fourteen-year-old girl was surely irresistible. I could hardly blame her for wanting to escape the cloud of my depression. I was a shadow of my former self, and I simply wasn't there for her.

But losing my daughter was a cruel twist, and it was around that time my doctor prescribed those sleeping pills.

Sophie lived with her father for almost eight months before they had a dreadful series of arguments and she returned to live with me. By then I had met Stuart and we'd just moved in together. I was so happy to have her back, but my joy was overshadowed by how troubled Sophie seemed at the time. She was quieter and more withdrawn than before. I put some of it down to normal teen reticence, but she seemed disturbed by something and I would often catch her watching us with a guarded look, as if she was deciding whether she could trust us.

Stuart and I were determined to make our life together work, and we did everything we could to help Sophie settle in. We developed new family routines, such as planning the following week's meals together each Thursday night. Sophie and Stuart shared a love for healthy food, but whenever I travelled away for work they would indulge in a McDonald's ice cream, teasing me for missing out on the treat. Watching the rapport that grew quickly between my daughter and my new love was heartening. Our lives were full, and a year later we moved cities. It felt like a fresh start for all of us. Stuart and I loved our new jobs and Sophie seemed happy in the new city. She occasionally travelled back to spend school holidays with her father and see her old friends, but she made some lovely friends at her new school, and even received a Young Achiever Award at the end of the first year.

⌒〜

I drew a deep breath and slowly shook my head as I looked across at the woman. "I really have no idea what triggered Sophie's drastic action last night." She nodded and put down her pen. She explained the rules of the ward then disappeared, returning a few minutes later with Sophie in her wake. My heart soared. Buoyed by a wave of overwhelming joy and relief to be with her once more, I ran forward and wrapped her up in my arms, hugging her close. It took me a few seconds to realise Sophie wasn't responding. I pulled back to look into her eyes but they were weary and vacant, looking past me as if I wasn't there. Her face was sullen, her body listless. My daughter was a shell of herself, and she displayed no sign of pleasure at my presence.

The woman gently indicated that we could have ten minutes alone while she waited outside.

I motioned Sophie toward the couch, gesturing for her to sit with me. She turned away and chose a chair on the other side of the room.

"Honey, how are you?" I asked, trying to keep my voice light.

With her feet tucked under her body and her eyes staring blankly towards an empty corner of the room, she didn't respond.

"Sophie, please talk to me." I leaned further forward hoping to draw her eyes towards mine, but she didn't move.

I felt my composure crumble and my voice became urgent; "Sophie, I need you to talk to me, darling."

Suddenly she glared at me. "Why couldn't you just let me die? The one thing I wanted and you couldn't even let me do that."

The shock knocked me back in the chair. Tears welled in my eyes as I responded, "Because I love you more than anything in the world, and my life is not worth living without you. Whatever you are going through, we can get you through it together."

"It's all about what *you* want. If you really gave a shit about me, you would have let me go!"

I felt the full force of her rage stab at my heart. This was not my gentle Sophie. I'd never seen her so angry. She was always a considerate girl, never pushing back or lashing out like this. The silence weighed heavy between us while I struggled to find the right words. I searched her face trying to understand what was going on in her mind, but I was at a loss, unsure what to say or do. "I will never let you go and I will never give up on you. I understand it doesn't feel that way at the moment, but I am your biggest supporter. I will do anything to help you through this, but I can't until you start talking."

"I don't want to talk! Please leave. I want you to leave." She got up and walked towards the door.

"Sophie, please, I need to help you! Don't walk away from me, not now." As she opened the door, I leapt up and threw my arms around her, holding tight and willing with all my might for her to respond, but her frail little body was unyielding. Then she pulled away.

As I watched her walk down the long empty corridor, I felt my world shatter in slow motion. I was defeated before I'd even had the chance to battle whatever anonymous enemy was stealing my daughter away.

She glanced back at me briefly, tears streaming down her face, then she rounded the corner. The impersonal click of the security door was followed by a hollow bang that reverberated like a gunshot straight through my heart.

Chapter 4
An Exorcism

"What do you mean you are discharging her?"

The call from the hospital asking me to come and pick Sophie up was unexpected. It was only day four. She didn't seem to be getting any better. Why would they do this?

My initial shock was replaced by pure panic. "She is a complete zombie. She can't even function. She's just a shell of her former self!"

I'd been visiting Sophie whenever I could, taking home-cooked meals and refusing to miss any of the visiting hours, hoping for the slightest sign she was ready to talk to me. At night Stuart came too, but she maintained her stubborn and accusatory silence. We were allowed to take her out of the ward to the McDonald's located on the lower level of the hospital one night for dinner. It didn't make any difference. In the middle of the restaurant she declared angrily, "I hate you both for not letting me die."

Her words cut cruelly, and so did her silence. Whatever brought her to this point was still a mystery to me, but I felt responsible. It was my job to keep my little girl safe. I should have known there was a problem before her pain grew too unbearable. Ignorance was no excuse. I had failed, and I felt guilty.

My attempts to engage her in conversation each day were fruitless. She appeared unchanged from the night she was admitted. Her eyes were still hollow and distant, her whole body weighed down by a heavy fatigue. She was like someone defeated, not wanting to surrender, but no longer able to find the energy to fight. It was heartbreaking to watch.

The voice on the end of the phone continued, "It's the medication she's on. It keeps her from harming herself, so she is now safe to be discharged. We only provide crisis care."

"But I don't understand. You haven't got to the heart of why she attempted suicide. And what is the plan to help her? Don't you have a plan?"

"She will have to be seen as an outpatient. You must make an appointment with the mental health service, but it could take several weeks or months."

"So what am I supposed to do? What if she does it again? How do I handle it? I don't know what to do," I exclaimed, struck by a sickening fear for my daughter's life.

"If she does it again you need to call the emergency number. The health service will work with you on how to handle it, but in the meantime you need to make your house safe. Take any sharp objects, ropes and harmful medication, even simple headache tablets, out of the house."

It was terrifying. I'd hardly slept for four days and I felt completely helpless. How could this be right? If they couldn't tell me how to fix it, where was I supposed to turn? I dragged myself to the shower and turned it on full strength, but as the water streamed down on my head, I felt the tight grip over my emotions slip. *Noooo, don't lose it now. If you do, it won't stop.* Every emotion I'd been holding back for the last few days rushed to the surface, a torrent stronger than the water flowing over my body. I could do nothing but surrender. Slumped against the shower wall, I wept deep, heaving sobs. It was an ugly cry that emerged without warning from some primal place. This emotion was one I'd never experienced before, but I instantly recognised it as the raw expression of my pain.

Time stood still while I hovered in an anguish-ridden limbo. My sobs exhaled the tension from my body, but in its place I felt no relief, only emptiness. When the water began to run cold, I became aware of my surroundings. The icy droplets stung my skin, calling me to attention; *Wake up! Pull yourself together, Rose.* I splashed my face with cold water one last time, and as I stepped out of the shower, I stared hard at my weary face in the mirror and gave myself a pep talk: *Your daughter needs you. What you do and say will make all the difference. You can get her through this, but you have to take control of yourself and take control of the situation. You are the parent, you know what your daughter needs. Don't sit back, you must act on your instinct. She needs you now more than ever.*

Before I left the house, I scoured each room for any sharp objects, cords and medication. Stuart helped me remove the blinds from Sophie's window, replacing them with a sheet secured by double sided tape. We packed all the knives, razors, scissors, belts, cords and pills into a box and put them into the boot of my car. When we finished, I felt strangely satisfied; *Phew, now I feel like I'm in control and able to keep my daughter safe from herself.* I was struck immediately by the absurdity of it all. *What the hell? Why on earth am I protecting her from herself? What is going on? How did she develop so much hatred towards herself that she would hack at the perfectly beautiful, amazing body I gave birth to almost seventeen years ago?*

⁓

Sophie was the most angelic and petite baby, with cute dimples framing a cheeky little smile. She was a delight for our whole family, and her older siblings were excited to have a happy doll to cuddle and carry in their clumsy little arms. She was always good-natured and accepting of the chaos in our household of lively children and working parents. It seemed to be in her nature right from the beginning to put other people's needs before her own, a trait I witnessed in her often. In fact, all my kids care greatly for those less fortunate, and I am so proud of their kindness.

When I first became a mother, I felt my heart burst with the deepest and most powerful love imaginable. All of a sudden life became bigger than me; I was a satellite circling a tiny defenceless human for whom I would lay down my life. When I was pregnant a few years later I wondered, *How could I ever love another baby this much?* Those worries dissolved the moment I gave birth. My daughter completed my world and I discovered the limitless love of motherhood.

Being a warm and loving mother with an unlimited supply of cuddles and kisses was important to me. My own mother struggled with that at times. It seemed I only truly won her approval when I got engaged. I was twenty-one when I married, and she took on the planning of my wedding with relish. I felt like I had finally passed one of her 'good daughter' tests. Little did she know that I saw the marriage, in some part, as a way of escaping from under the cloud of her disapproval.

Even as a young girl she would tell me I was a disappointment. "Why can't you dress like the other girls?" she would ask. She displayed few soft edges at home, saving her best behaviour for the outside world. She seemed determined to portray herself as the perfect mother with the perfect family, but behind closed doors she flew off the handle often. There were beltings, but it was the cutting words that left scars; "You are such a disappointment. I am so ashamed of you."

When I was around eleven years old, my parents joined a local minister who created his own 'born again' religion. The weekly services terrified me. I had been transported from Sunday rituals in the local Uniting Church, where the mood was calm and the voices low, to a place where I was surrounded by adults speaking in tongues and collapsing to the floor. They would acclaim in loud cries that Jesus or the Holy Spirit had entered their body. I couldn't understand how any of it related to the god I'd been raised to believe in.

One evening, not long after our move to the new church, my mother and I had a huge fight. Eleven seemed to be my age of rebellion. That's when I remember first openly defying her, my growing resentment somehow finding its voice. Despite my bravado, I lay awake all night in fear, knowing my mother would not let my rebellion go unpunished. In the morning, Mum said nothing about it and I climbed into the car to go shopping with her. On the way, she pulled up outside a house I'd never seen before. The ramshackle weatherboard home with flaking paint and a tarnished tin roof was similar to all the other unremarkable homes lining the unexceptional streets in our suburb. I could see the minister standing on the wide front porch and he appeared to be waiting for us. I wondered if Mum was here to collect something. I followed her up the wide creaking stairs and he led us into the house. He turned right into the front room and my mother gestured for me to follow, but when the door clicked closed behind me, I realised the minister was there, but not my mother.

I was scared, but he told me not to be afraid and to sit on a large chair placed right in the middle of the room. It was made from dark wood and had a high, solid back. In better times you might almost say it was regal, but the cushion embedded into the seat was faded and the solid wood armrests were scratched and worn. I sat, obedient but wary. The stale, musty smell in my nostrils reminded me of visits to my grandmother's home. Thin, yellowing curtains hung loosely across the windows, allowing only a pale light into the room. Apart from the big chair, the room appeared to be empty except for a small stool in front of me and a little table with a dish of water to the side.

The minister bent forward, bringing his face close to mine. He was probably in his late thirties, with fair hair and penetrating blue eyes that scanned my own. Every Sunday I'd watched him perform from a distance, his undeniable charisma whipping his flock into a frenzy, but this was the first time I had been so close, and the first time he had directed his hypnotic gaze toward me.

"You are possessed by the devil," he declared. "I will exorcise Satan from you and let the Holy Spirit enter your body." I froze. I wanted to run back to my mother, but was too afraid to move.

He threw his hands up in the air and began speaking in tongues. His voice grew louder and louder until he was screaming, commanding Satan to leave me in the name of Jesus Christ! His fingers occasionally dipped into the dish of what I imagine was holy water, which he flicked above my head, letting it rain down on me. I couldn't believe what I was seeing and my little heart pounded. I could hardly breathe, pushing my back hard against the chair and trying desperately to vanish into the creases of the unforgiving cushion.

It seemed to go on forever, but then I yawned and he screamed with delight, "That's the devil coming right out of you now."

I remember thinking, *You idiot, it's not the devil. It's a yawn because I'm tired.* Even though his ranting performance left me unimpressed, the incident left its mark on me. It was the first time I remember feeling shame; a poisonous emotion that makes you doubt yourself and hide your true nature away. If my mother thought she must bring me to a scary place to have something removed by God himself, I must be deeply flawed.

The following year I was sent to boarding school. From the moment I arrived I wrote letters every day pleading with my parents to let me come home. I couldn't bear the feeling of being banished. Under different circumstances, I think the whole boarding school experience would have suited me, but I was already so heightened to the emotional withdrawal of my mother that I wasn't able to consider my new surroundings in a positive light. My letters had no effect, even with the addition of a few well-placed tears to blur the ink. Realising I would need a new approach, I went on a hunger strike. It took the school staff a while to notice, but they eventually called my parents and insisted someone come. My mother made the three-hour trip the next day and took me out of the school. I was so relieved. My parents really did care! We stayed for a few nights with my grandmother, where I enjoyed my new-found appetite and the rare opportunity to spend time alone with my mum. Eager to return home, I asked her when we would leave. That's when she told me she was heading home at the end of the week and I would be going back to the boarding school.

It was a crushing blow, and it beat the last remnant of my childhood belief in fairytales right out of me. I had been abandoned. No one would come to rescue me from the castle tower, or fight the dragon, or recognise the princess hidden beneath the servant clothing. If I wasn't to be someone's princess adorned in silk and diamonds, I would shun all those fantasies. I became goth-like: black clothes, black eyeliner, black nail polish and a black mood. I went into a cocoon, hiding away the last traces of my bright, sparkling personality. I stopped entertaining my vibrantly coloured dreams as well as my last shreds of hope for a warm and loving family.

Pulling up outside the hospital to collect Sophie, I was determined she should never feel the same sense of desertion and neglect. No matter what befalls any of my children, to me they are perfect and I will love them without judgement until my last breath.

We travelled home in silence. The young lady beside me was barely recognisable. I could still feel her projected hostility, even though her eyes were glazed and her movements sluggish. When we arrived home, she ignored Stuart and went straight up to her room. We'd chosen the house because the whole upstairs area was like a teen retreat. Sophie had a bedroom, bathroom and living space all to herself. The separation and privacy seemed such a wonderful idea a year earlier when we moved in, but our home no longer felt like a safe haven. The space upstairs terrified me. I couldn't see or hear Sophie, and I worried constantly whether I'd missed something. *Did I pull the drawers in her bathroom out far enough to be sure nothing was hiding there? Was there something in a dark corner of her wardrobe I hadn't seen? Could some ordinary item I assumed was safe, actually be lethal?*

Stuart tried to reassure me that Sophie would be alright, but we were both on edge. We tiptoed quietly as if walking on eggshells, and spoke in muffled whispers. We didn't want her to hear our worried voices and notice how ill-equipped we felt about having her home.

I struggled to settle, prowling in circles around the house. I picked things up then put them down again; I mindlessly checked emails; I tried to prepare dinner. Whenever I became engrossed in any of these activities, my heart skipped violently and my mind scolded me harshly; *you don't know what she's doing!* Then I'd fly upstairs with some feeble excuse: "Do you want some dinner?" "Would you like some water?" "How are you feeling?" "I've made an appointment for you with the doctor." It wasn't normal for me, but none of us were normal now. My anxiety knew only one thing; to constantly make sure Sophie was safe. I couldn't resist the call deep in my belly to confirm it with my own eyes.

Each time I ventured into her room, Sophie met my pathetic attempts for reassurance with, "Leave me alone," or, "Piss off!" I backed away and gently closed the door each time, but it was never long before I returned. I was convinced that only my presence could ward off danger.

Before we retired to bed, I went out to my car where I had left her medication. I carried the night's dose along with a glass of water up to her room. Sitting on her bed, I waited for her to take it, all the time watching her throat to see if she swallowed. I resisted the temptation to ask her to open her mouth so I could be sure it went down. I was scared if I did that, it would tip her over the edge. In fact, I was scared anything I said or did would tip her over the edge. When I reached the door, I suddenly remembered the glass; *Oh shit.* I turned back and picked it up. "I love you more than anything in the world, honey," I said, hoping to distract her from my action, but I could see she knew why I was taking the glass out of her room …

~

As I folded my exhausted body down on the bed that night, I could feel the pounding of my heart. I knew sleep was not going to come easy. Unbearable scenes of Sophie hurting herself drifted through my mind. I pictured her blood-stained figure looming over me and I wondered if she would come to stir me next time. Her anger convinced me I wouldn't get a second chance. I needed to stay alert.

Stuart pulled me close, but the warm cocoon created by his enveloping arms, usually so soothing, could not break the spell. "Rose, we will get through this. We will both do whatever it takes to get her through whatever is troubling her." Even if *I* believed that, I didn't think *she* did. She hated us. How could we get her through this if she didn't trust us?

Sensing my anxiety, Stuart encouraged me to take long slow breaths and talked me through a relaxation sequence we had learnt together years earlier. His soft, low voice coaxed forth the vision of our happy place, the magical beach where we married. I could see the deep blue ocean and streaks of white-tipped waves endlessly melting in delicate lacy swirls on a long shoreline. The wide expanse of soft, golden sand snakes its way north, but my attention turns south towards the weathered rocks scattered like sentinels below a rising headland. It's where we pledged our love. The rhythmic rumble of the waves breaking on the rocks is what truly soothes me. It is not so much heard with the ears, but felt deep in the heart.

Normally I can stay with the vision, suspended above like a hovering bird in the fresh sea breeze. Normally I can soak in the beauty and feel my muscles relax. Normally I can fall asleep within minutes, but not that night. I couldn't hold onto it. My world had contracted to the space upstairs where Sophie lay. My mind was enslaved by the need to protect her. I didn't care about my exhaustion, my pain, my hunger or my comfort. There would be no more 'me' for a very long time.

⁓

Stuart fell into a deep sleep but my mind would give me no peace. *If I just go up and check on her, I'll be able to go to sleep.* Slipping quietly out of bed, I tiptoed upstairs to her room and gently opened the door. The moonlight fell brightly on the sheet we used to cover her window, casting a tile of light across her body. I stood beside her bed, captivated by her angelic beauty as I had been so many times since she was a baby. My heart was filled with immense love, but also too much pain and sadness. And questions, so many questions I was too afraid to ask. Tears fell from my cheek, threatening to land on her face in the same way hers had landed on mine just a few nights ago. Was she feeling as desperately lost on that fateful night as I was now? I felt helpless. I didn't know how to help her or what to do. But I hadn't lost hope, and I would need to carry enough of it now for both of us.

Back in bed I still couldn't sleep. While she seemed to be resting peacefully, I was petrified she would get up and harm herself. I grabbed my pillow and a doona from the linen cupboard in the hallway and crept back upstairs. Sliding stealthily into her bed, I lay listening to her deep, slow breaths. I couldn't resist reaching out to run my fingers through her long golden hair, letting the fine tendrils brush my fingertips. It seemed like only yesterday I was nursing my pure and innocent baby girl.

Sophie stirred, waking enough to notice I was there. "I don't want you here. Just piss off," she mumbled, her tone groggy but unforgiving. I drew back quickly, shaken by her stark reminder that my presence brought her no comfort. I hesitated for a moment, knowing she didn't want me there, but feeling unable to leave. I knew I'd never sleep if I was not near her, so I spread the doona on the floor outside her bedroom door and curled up. *If she comes to any harm, I will be where I need to be.* This would be my bed for many nights in the coming months.

Chapter 5
The Letter

On the day Sophie tried to take her own life, 178 other Australians also attempted suicide. Eight of them died.*

⌒

One week after Sophie returned home, our lives were still on hold. She sheltered in her room; I slept outside her door; Stuart crept quietly around the house. The silence was heavy and I felt a nauseous sense of apprehension that wouldn't go away.

A visit to our local doctor convinced us the best course of action would be to admit Sophie to a private mental health clinic, but my calls to each of them were met with the same response: "I'm sorry, our beds are full. We can add your daughter to our waiting list, but it is likely to be about three months before a place becomes available."

We couldn't wait a few months. The medication was having a massive effect on Sophie. She was groggy and extremely low. It was devastating to see her this way. Her beautiful, young soul was completely empty, as if someone had sucked all the life out of her. Something needed to change fast.

Sleep evaded me, so a few nights after I'd exhausted my efforts with the clinics, I crept downstairs and grabbed my computer. I'd lived a privileged life, but now I felt powerless. This was the first time I'd been at a complete loss about how to fix something. I couldn't simply sit around and wait; it's not in my nature. Instead I began to write. I typed frantically, unsure exactly who would read these words, but believing there must be someone with the power to help my daughter, if only I could get a message through to them ...

I find myself in a desperate situation that I would give anything not to be in, and nor should any parent.

Last Sunday evening my beautiful daughter attempted suicide. I found myself looking at a lifeless empty soul who was once the most vivacious, determined and intelligent young lady. Just last year she received a young achievers award at her school.

While my life since last Sunday has literally been a living nightmare, I find myself totally helpless. She was taken to the closest hospital where she was later admitted to their mental health ward. The staff, specialists and paramedics have been tremendous.

Her care has been good, but the public hospital can only offer crisis care. We have therefore researched our options to get her the professional and intense help she desperately needs – this is when my immense feeling of utter helplessness and despair spiralled further. As a parent I am used to doing, and should be able to do, whatever it takes to provide for my children, but I find I cannot.

We have her on several waiting lists at private clinics and we are still waiting. The staff are inundated daily by desperate loved ones with no beds or vacancies to offer them. It is nothing but gut wrenching! And we are the 'lucky ones' who can afford private health. What happens to all our fellow Australians who can't afford this 'necessity'? We would sell everything we own to get her the help she needs, but sadly even money isn't enough.

My main priority at the moment is to get my daughter better. Once we have her there, my husband and I have vowed to do all it takes to stop this tragic epidemic. Too many people are taken by this senseless and insidious disease.

Please remember my name because I will be standing up and making sure every politician, every health professional and every fellow Australian listens, takes notice and stands up with us to save our future generation and eliminate youth suicide. I know there is no easy or quick fix, which is why it is so important we all join together. I will not stop.

Yours truly

My desperate plea was more than a cry for help. I was appalled that in 2017, in a country as lucky as Australia, anyone would have to wait for help when they were at death's door. It shouldn't matter whether the danger was from oneself, or from a disease, or from another person; we must be able to rise in support of our most vulnerable. We pride ourselves on living in a safe and advanced country, one where people in other parts of the world aspire to live, but I had stumbled onto our weak underbelly. Our most vulnerable were often alone in their struggles. I couldn't let it happen to Sophie, and I don't believe we should let it happen to anyone.

I had no plan but I had to chase every possible lead. Anything less would have felt like giving up. Finishing the letter, I decided to go straight to the top. I sent it to the Prime Minister of Australia, the local Premier, and the founder of Beyond Blue, Australia's well-known mental health support organisation. I whispered a furtive prayer as I pressed the send button, but the whoosh of the departing emails seemed to punctuate my sense of hopelessness. I hardened myself to the likelihood that the best I might receive from my desperate act would be a letter a few weeks later.

The next day at exactly 9am my phone rang. "Rose, it's Jeff Kennett from Beyond Blue. How are you and how is your daughter?" When I heard his name I wept. I think we all want to believe someone out there will respond to our desperate cries for help. Jeff's voice was like a strong hand reaching into the pit of my despair and hauling me out.

I explained how we had Sophie on every waitlist with every private mental health clinic in the city. Jeff said, "Give me an hour, Rose, and I'll see what I can do." Within the hour I received a phone call from the very first clinic I'd tried a few days earlier. They advised me they could offer a place for Sophie and asked me to bring her in that afternoon.

My relief was overwhelming. I didn't spare a moment wondering how Jeff achieved the breakthrough, I was just so grateful. In a few short days I'd discovered how little I understood about the world of mental health services. We were now totally dependent on the mass of mental health workers whose roles I had never fully understood, and the kindness of strangers like Jeff who recognised in us their own journey of confusion and fear. Most of us will only discover this hidden world of remarkable people when something goes wrong, but it's when our lives are going right that we should know of them, support them and be part of creating a stronger safety net for each and every human.

⌒

We had momentum, but I knew there was one last hurdle; Sophie was still stubbornly silent, not speaking more than a few words to us since coming home. I couldn't be sure she would buy into the plan.

Apprehensively I went into her room and sat on the end of her bed. I explained that I had written a letter to some powerful people pleading for their help. Then I told her about Jeff's call and his remarkable concern for us. While I spoke I watched her intently, trying to read her reaction, but it was impossible.

"Sophie, a wonderful clinic just phoned and they would like you to come up today at 4pm. I know it's going to be difficult, but we need to get you the best help we can. I would like you to at least give this a shot."

She looked up at me with tears welling in her sunken eyes. A deep sadness was written all over her face, and as she replied, a few huge tears spilled down her sweet little cheeks. "Mum, I can't do this anymore. I have nothing left. I don't know if I can get through it."

It was the first crack I'd seen since everything began. There was my brave girl reaching out through the tiniest chink in the armour she had built around herself. She wanted so much to do what I asked, but I could see she doubted her own strength.

"Please, baby, I'm begging you to please give this a try. I promise I will be there with you every step of the way for whatever you need."

"I don't know ..."

My mouth quivered, then my own tears flowed fast. I reached out and grabbed her hands, declaring loudly, "I will never give up on you. Do you hear me? I will never give up on you! I love you more than anything and my life is not worth living without you. So, if you have any ounce of love for me, you will not give up on yourself either and you will at least try."

I was hysterical and Stuart came running into the room. He'd heard my raised voice and he instantly saw how upset we both were. The moment the words had been uttered, I was struck by a cold fear. *Had I gone too far? Would this push her over the edge? What have I done!*

I looked up at Stuart through the blur of my tears, pleading silently for him to help. He took a deep breath, came over to the bed and gently lay down beside Sophie. He gestured for me to join them.

Softly he asked, "Sophie, how do you feel about giving it a go?"

Still crying, she responded, "I don't want to be like this, but I don't know if I've got anything left."

"Well, honey, how about we take it one day at a time, even one moment at a time – baby steps. Mum and I will be there with you every step of the way."

"Okay," she said hesitantly, but without the angry resistance of the last few days.

Saying nothing more, Stuart and I simply wrapped her more tightly in our arms. For a moment I allowed myself to savour a jumble of sweet sensations as my daughter finally let me hold her close.

Sophie didn't have the energy to pack her bag so I gathered what I thought she would need – pyjamas, toiletries and of course her Ted.

Ted is a pale pink blanket with a big teddy bear stitched into it, made by her great-aunt when Sophie was a baby. She carried it everywhere, clasping the blanket around the top under Ted's head and often sucking her thumb at the same time. Sophie was a placid little baby, but she could also be quite anxious and clingy. Holding Ted would always soothe her.

One night when she was barely a toddler, I went out to dinner with some girlfriends while her father stayed with the children. When I arrived home Sophie was laying in her cot sobbing in her sleep. My heart sank. *What could have upset my poor little baby so much that she was sobbing, even in her sleep?* I grabbed Ted, picked her up and sat in the chair nursing her for more than an hour until her sobbing subsided and she settled. Later, when I asked him what happened, her father said she was being a sook because I wrapped the kids up in cotton wool – of course it was all my fault.

At 4pm we walked into the foyer of the clinic. We were all nervous, not knowing what to expect. I filled out the forms and they explained the fee structure. I looked at Stuart, but he shrugged and said "Rose, we have to do what we have to do. Don't worry about the money." I was prepared to pay anything to get her the help she needed, but I was still concerned. Stuart and I both came to our relationship with very little. Stuart had always paid child support and more for his boys, but I received nothing from Sophie's father.

We were taken to the ward and shown into a room that would be Sophie's home for the next two weeks. It was very simple with a single bed, a cupboard and an ensuite. The walls were painted a neutral off-white colour and the view from the tinted window revealed a concrete jungle of hospital buildings. The room seemed unfinished, then I noticed there were no power points or lamps, not even curtains; only a tiny TV wired straight into the wall sitting high in a corner. The sombre room with its smell of bleach reminded me this was a hospital and Sophie was here because she was too sick to remain at home.

A nurse asked us to open Sophie's bag so she could check her belongings. She removed the phone charger, explaining it was not allowed in the room and would be kept at the nurses' station. She wasn't allowed to have many ordinary things such as pens or even her favourite mug I'd packed next to Ted. I realised they had to remove anything a patient could use to harm themselves. I would soon become all too accustomed to noticing such details and scanning constantly for these new forms of danger.

Once Sophie was settled we were told to say our goodbyes. I didn't want to leave her. The sadness in her eyes pulled at my heartstrings. Had I left my child in the best possible hands?

At home that night I slept in my own bed. I fell quickly into a heavy slumber, but after a few hours I woke. Lying quietly in the dark so as not to disturb Stuart, I contemplated the sudden change in our lives. It was my first opportunity to reflect on the last few weeks without feeling the frantic urge to do something, but the anxiety still fluttered in my chest like the wings of a butterfly unable to land.

My office was just a few blocks from the clinic and I was eager to visit Sophie after work the next day. I thought of her constantly, hoping her first day might miraculously deliver some results, but deep down I knew I shouldn't expect progress that quickly.

During the day I received a phone call from Sophie's treating psychiatrist. Dr Rama spoke softly, but there was also a detached professionalism in her voice. I was struggling to understand all the different roles of the people at the clinic, and I was wary. Every time I thought I might get some answers, I was confronted with more questions. I had no clue whether we were on the right track or not. Dr Rama clearly sensed my anxiety and reassured me Sophie's safety and health was her priority. Once she finished assessing Sophie over the coming days she wanted Stuart and I to come in for a family meeting, and she would also have one over the phone with Sophie's father.

As soon as I could escape the office, I dashed to the clinic. Navigating the security protocols and showing the identification tag I'd been given when Sophie checked in, I walked quickly through the corridors to the door of her room. Opening it slowly, I could see her lying on the bed staring at the ceiling. I took a deep breath, checked my smile was in place, then walked over to the bed and gently put my arms around her.

"How was your day, baby?" I asked as I scanned her pale face.

"I'm tired. I don't want to talk about it," she replied.

I retreated to the seat against the wall. "How are you feeling?"

"Mum, I feel like shit and I said I don't want to talk about it."

Alright, if she doesn't want to talk about her day, I'll tell her about mine. I prattled lightly about the traffic, my new assistant at work, a favourite song I'd heard on the radio, anything to distract her from her worries for a while, but she wasn't interested. When I ran out of stories, we sat in silence. I didn't mind. I wanted her to know I was there for her, that she wasn't alone. But it wasn't all about her. Being there was the only way to keep my fears at bay.

When it was time to leave, I leant over and kissed her gently on the forehead. I walked toward the door, then looked back and said, "Three squeezes, baby."

The slightest whisper of a smile touched her lips and she said, "Four back."

My heart leapt and I floated down the corridor with a wide smile on my face. This was our own secret language, a family tradition that originated many years ago when Sophie's older brother told me, "I'm a big boy now mum, you have to stop telling me you love me in front of all my mates." He was six years old.

⌒

We were walking home from school, me pushing Sophie in her pram while her older brother jumped and skipped along beside us. He was in his second year, and at that age school was like one big play date. His animated little face beamed as he regaled me with stories from the day. Just before we reached home, my little man announced he was too old now for me to call out 'I love you' in front of his friends. I'll never forget the bittersweet feeling. I was so proud watching him grow up, but I didn't want him to break up with me! I understood how important his friends were and that he needed space to grow, but for me it was important for my children to hear I loved them whenever we parted. So I came up with a compromise – every time I left him I grabbed his hand and squeezed it three times. The three squeezes meant *I. Love. You.* It wasn't long before he started squeezing my hand back four times, telling me, "Mum, it means I love you too." Gosh that little man made my heart melt.

The next year he decided he was too big to even hold my hand. "But if I can't hold your hand, how am I going to tell you I love you?" I asked.

"It's easy, Mum, you say *three squeezes* to me and I will say *four back*."

And so began our special love language, adopted by the whole family. Even now as adults, we never end a phone conversation or part ways without saying it.

Chapter 6
What About the Sex?

"How's your relationship?" Dr Rama dived straight into her questions as soon as we took a seat in her office. Stuart and I looked quizzically at each other, not because we didn't know the answer to the question, but because we'd been caught off guard. We expected questions about Sophie, not about us.

"Great!" we both nodded.

"What about the sex?" This time I couldn't hold back a scandalised gasp. Meeting Dr Rama had allowed me to put a face to the voice and she wasn't what I expected. Her gentle eyes and soft smooth skin made it difficult to pick her age. I guessed she couldn't be much older than me. When we shook hands I noticed how small and fragile hers was within my firm grip. Dressed plainly in loose-fitting clothes, I couldn't initially associate the motherly woman before me with the crisp professional on the phone a week earlier. However, she was making it quite clear who was in control of the interview. Whenever she spoke, she watched us with an intensity I found intimidating. I felt like she was constantly assessing our reactions. Of course, she was. That was her job.

I took a sneaky glance at Stuart just as he declared, "Our sex life is great!"

"Yes, we have sex," I mumbled quietly.

Stuart and I did have sex; we had great sex. In fact our sex was the best sex I'd ever had. We were so in love. We trusted each other implicitly and were vulnerable with each other. It took our intimacy to a level I'd never experienced before. When we reached that point in our relationship, I knew I'd be with him forever. Knowing each other's bodies and pleasure points so intimately was magical. For us, sex was an act of pure love.

The twenty years I spent with Sophie's father was the exact opposite. He said the only way he could feel my love was through sex, but there was no tenderness in his touch, just expectation and demand. He used sex as a weapon, at times saying I didn't love him if I didn't give him sex every day. I felt trapped. I'd been with him since I was eighteen years old and I didn't know what was normal. *Maybe there is something wrong with me,* I would often think. He would ridicule my attempts to avoid his advances, calling me names and laughing at me. Looking back, I can see how it ate away at my self-confidence. In other parts of my life I was a real dynamo, but in the bedroom I experienced so much self-doubt. Most of the time I would go along with his sexual approaches to appease him. I quickly learnt to pretend I enjoyed it, then it would be over a lot sooner and I could avoid his verbal insults. But in the end, avoiding his demeaning words meant I was tolerating his demeaning touch and enabling his abuse. Experiencing the tender and respectful relationship with Stuart made me recognise how abnormal my first marriage had been.

Dr Rama leaned forward and paused, her direct gaze drilling deep into my eyes. She turned her head slowly to look at Stuart, then back to me. "Are you," she articulated precisely but slowly, "involved in *other* extramarital activities?"

She looked directly into my eyes and I could feel my brow crumple in confusion as I stared back at her. Why on earth would she be asking us this? I turned to Stuart. His face wore the same lost and bewildered look. "No, of course not!" we responded in unison.

She leaned back in her chair, and while I didn't yet know Dr Rama, I'm pretty sure she looked relieved. Taking a deep breath, she explained that Sophie's father had been insinuating Stuart and I were involved in improper behaviours with other people. I knew he'd been trying to convince friends and family members I was an unfit mother since our separation, but I never understood how far he'd taken it. With this revelation, Sophie's apparent wariness when she first came to live with us began to make sense. The time with her father had left her more vulnerable to the animosity of our separation than I'd realised. It was confirmation that my silence around the disgraceful behaviour of her father had been a mistake. He'd been using it against me when it should have been him who was ashamed and humiliated. It made me so angry.

"My God, how dare he do this. I caught him years ago leading another life with all these strangers, having sex and doing depraved acts with both men and women, having orgies and whatever else they did!"

I couldn't believe I blurted that out to her. I had hidden the episode from everyone for years before telling Stuart quite early in our relationship. He'd convinced me to tell my parents, who had repeatedly accused me of not trying hard enough to hold my family together. They even threw their support behind their son-in-law, giving him a place to stay when I refused to let him return home. Hiding that dirty secret caused me plenty of pain and anguish, not only then, but for many years to come.

It was Easter 2010.

The business I had founded seven years earlier grew fast, but I was feeling the strain. I was trying to be a full-time mother while juggling nearly thirty staff and a constant stream of issues. There was no downtime, and even our holidays were interrupted by work. On this particular Easter we were away with friends, but a client needed my help. That's why, early on Good Friday morning while everyone slept late, I quickly threw on some clothes and grabbed my car keys. *I'll be back before they wake,* I told myself as I commenced the one-hour drive to my office in the early dawn light.

The office was in a factory I'd built just a year after starting the business. Even though the weight of business ownership was heavy, I was proud to have created the manufacturing company from scratch. It was a source of security and financial freedom for my family. My children all attended great schools, we'd bought our dream home, and I'd employed my husband to run the day-to-day management of the factory.

Arriving at the office, I noticed his computer was still on. Rather than wait for mine to start up, I jumped into his chair and shuffled the mouse to wake up his screen. Images slowly came into focus and I realised I was looking at some sort of chat site. It didn't take me long to comprehend it was also a sex site. He'd been engaging in conversations with someone … no, with many people! The room began to spin. As I read some of the messages, it became apparent he had been meeting these people regularly, both women and men, for what they were calling 'daytime plays'. They wrote lurid and depraved descriptions of what they did to each other and what they planned to do next. The messages went back six years. A layer of sweat broke out across my skin and the room went dim. I didn't know whether I would faint or throw up. Clasping my head in my hands, I waited for the waves of nausea to pass. When I lifted my head, I hit the print button over and over and over again.

Dr Rama's line of questioning now made sense. He had been rewriting his own history as if it was mine. He knew I printed the pages from his computer, but he also knew I hadn't told anyone at the time. I convinced myself I needed to remain silent to protect my children from the damage it would surely cause them to discover their father's disgusting behaviour, but the truth is, I was paralysed by a humiliating sense of shame and disgust, not just in him, but in myself. How had I married someone like that?

Dr Rama gently touched my hand. "Rose, from what Sophie told me and from what you have explained, I believe you have suffered your own trauma. I'm not your psychiatrist and I cannot treat you, but I encourage you to seek help too."

I knew she was right. I'd never sought help to deal with my emotional turmoil. By the time I discovered his deception, I was already hurting in ways I had never acknowledged. He had an affair a decade earlier and I took him back. He labelled me frigid and I accepted his judgement. He slyly, almost imperceptibly, undermined me, mocked me and criticised me until I no longer knew who I was.

⌒

When I left the office with those pages detailing his appalling betrayal stuffed into an envelope, I couldn't go back and face him. I couldn't face anyone. I got in my car and stared blankly at the factory wall for what seemed like hours. I finally picked up the phone and called him. "I found it; the vile stuff on your computer." I recall the alarm in his voice when he realised what I was saying. He begged me to wait until he came home, but I interrupted him, "No, I don't want to see you! Stay there with the children. When you come back, I want you to pack your bags and leave." Then I turned my car for home.

Alone, locked away in the house for the rest of the long weekend, I rode waves of emotion, horrified to discover something so depraved had occurred right under my nose. I got drunk and wept pathetic tears of self-pity. I got angry and pulled all our photos off the wall. I wandered from room to room haunted by a feeling of wretched loss as I picked up my children's clothes and held them to my face so I could inhale their sweet smell. I was outraged that he would expose us to such a disgusting and dangerous world. Anger was, strangely enough, the most soothing of all my emotions, making me feel strong, righteous and determined to end the marriage. But despair returned quickly, and with it, a paralysing belief in exactly what he'd told me so many times – I couldn't make it on my own. I couldn't stay with him, but I couldn't bear the thought of uprooting my children from their home. I couldn't see any way out.

Two years later my business was gone. Despite my efforts to keep our family life together for the sake of our children, nothing could erase my mistrust and disgust for him. It eventually became greater than my fear of leaving him.

Telling Dr Rama about my sordid past was cathartic in many ways, but now was not the time to deal with my problems. This was about Sophie and I was desperate to understand what we faced. Dr Rama told us her interviews with Sophie and the background she had uncovered in the last few days led her to a diagnosis of post-traumatic stress disorder (PTSD), also suffering anxiety and depression. While the cause was not clear, I was relieved we at least had a diagnosis. But Dr Rama was not finished. "Because Sophie is sixteen years old and no longer considered a minor, it is not possible for me to reveal any details to you." My relief evaporated. Just as the picture was beginning to reveal itself, we were once again left with questions unanswered and more secrets to unravel. I felt the weight of helplessness descend like a heavy cloak, but Dr Rama's next words will stay with me forever: "Rose and Stuart, you need to understand that Sophie is standing on the edge of a cliff. She is very vulnerable and at an extremely high risk of suicide. How you handle this and respond will make all the difference."

Standing on the edge of a cliff. It made sense of why I was scared of every little thing I said and did around her, and why I was gripped by fear whenever I was away from her. Her life was on a knife edge, precarious, vulnerable to the smallest shifts in fortune. I could see Sophie wilting before my eyes, and I didn't think it would take much to tip her off that cliff. One wrong word, one mindless moment, and I might never see my daughter again.

~

Stuart and I agreed to let Sophie share with us when she was ready, and to never ask her or put pressure on her to divulge anything. I didn't want to risk causing her more distress, plus I was terrified of being the one whose words might push her over. But if I'm honest, I was also nervous about what she would reveal. Could I handle it? Whatever had dragged my daughter to the edge of a cliff must be bad. I wavered between the desperate need to know exactly what she was struggling with, and my concern that I would not be able to cope with her revelations.

Dr Rama told us she had already interviewed Sophie's father and concluded he was not a good support for Sophie; he could even be a danger to her recovery. She directed him not to contact Sophie or the clinic during her treatment. I never considered he would ever be a threat to his own children. What did that mean? But Dr Rama moved on.

"Stuart, how do you feel about Sophie?" she asked.

"I love her like she's my own. She's a massive part of Rose, actually the spitting image of her – a part of the package, I would say. It has been extremely difficult going through all of this. I try not to get involved. I leave all the decisions and disciplining up to Rose and her father, because I'm not her parent. But I am also here to support Rose and her children in any way I can."

She continued taking notes, then looked up.

"Stuart, are you willing and able to stand up and be the father figure in her life?"

"Of course," Stuart responded without hesitation. "I will do whatever it takes to help Sophie."

"You need to show her unconditional love, the same as you do with your sons. You need to set boundaries and even discipline her when needed, while also showing her you still love her no matter what. She has never been given healthy, unconditional love from her father. She desperately needs that."

We left the meeting feeling overwhelmed. I'd arrived believing Dr Rama would shed light on Sophie's desperate act and why she had inexplicably found herself engaged in a life or death battle, but we were leaving with more questions than answers. The next steps were a mystery and I was in the worst place possible for someone like me – totally out of control.

⌒‿

For two weeks I visited Sophie twice a day. Gradually I noticed slight improvements, but it was achingly slow. There were days when I walked into her room and could feel the heaviness of her pain in the air. Her eyes were sad and empty like she was grieving. I wore my smile each time I entered her room and I celebrated inside whenever I was able to stir a positive response from her. She would occasionally smile weakly at one of my jokes, or ask me about my day. That she displayed enough mental energy to even wonder what was happening in life outside the clinic seemed like progress to me.

One day I arrived to find her sitting up expectantly on her bed with half a smile on her face. "Mum, Dr Rama said I could come home for dinner tomorrow night. Can you pick me up after work?"

"Of course. How exciting! What would you like for dinner? I'll cook whatever you want."

"Can we have your honey soy chicken with fried rice?" she asked. At last I could see a glimpse of happiness in her eyes. "We certainly can," I nodded, determined to do anything to help her stay positive.

The following day wouldn't go fast enough. I rushed into work early and bounced around ticking things off my list. My team made sure nothing held me back from leaving right on time. After weeks of putting on a brave face at work, my optimism was finally genuine, and I felt them reciprocate with real excitement about this small step forward. When I reached her room, Sophie was ready to go and we quickly completed the paperwork necessary for her to leave the building. It felt amazing to have her beside me in the car – ordinary, but in the circumstances, so extraordinary. It was these everyday little moments I desperately wanted back in my life, and as we slowly rolled along in the peak hour traffic, I could see her peering curiously at the passing scene like a traveller returned home from a long time abroad.

"Mum," she said, still looking out the window of the car, "I don't want you to bring me back to the clinic tonight. Can Stuart take me back?"

"Okay, whatever you prefer," I replied, curious but unwilling to probe the reason for her very specific request.

When we walked through the door she went straight to her bedroom and I followed her up the stairs. I was too afraid to let her out of my sight. It was worse than having a newborn baby. *At least a newborn cannot harm themselves*, I thought wryly. I tried to hide my anxiety as she wandered around her room touching things and pulling a few extra clothes out of her wardrobe. After about ten minutes I asked her to come down and help me cook dinner.

When Stuart walked through the door, Sophie ran up and gave him the biggest hug. I felt the tension leave my body, knowing he would help me keep an eye on her now. They sat on the couch and chatted while I finished making dinner.

Sitting around the dinner table enjoying a simple meal together was amazing. Our home felt warm and cosy, and for the first time since that fateful night when I'd woken to her shadowy figure leaning over me, I believed everything might turn out okay.

When the time came to take Sophie back to the clinic she jumped up and said, "Stuart, can you please take me back? I don't want Mum to come, only you."

"Of course, let me get my keys," he replied, looking over the top of her head and into my eyes with a questioning smile. I shrugged, genuinely unaware what she was planning, but comfortable these two were safe together.

When they reached the door, I wrapped Sophie in a long hug, hiding my face in her hair and wanting the moment to last forever. I kissed her beautiful smooth forehead and whispered in her ear, "Three squeezes, baby."

"Four back, Mum."

After they left, I poured myself a glass of wine and sat out on the back patio in the cool autumn air. A moment alone to savour our lovely night together was a sweet pleasure. I imagined future nights when we could sit together without the fear and anxiety that now seemed to be my constant companion. I wanted my gorgeous girl to be happy and I couldn't rest until she was.

Before long my phone rang. It was Stuart. "Honey," he blurted, his voice cracking with emotion.

Terrified, I replied, "What is it?"

"Sophie just asked me to be her dad!"

"What? What happened?"

"We were driving along and she said Dr Rama told her she needed a real father figure in her life, someone who would show her unconditional love. She said she wants someone who she loves and respects, and who she can look up to. Then she asked me if I would be that man – her Dad."

Since that day, she has only called him 'Dad'. I would occasionally mention to someone that Stuart was her stepdad, but Sophie would correct me; "No, Mum, he *is* my dad and that is that." And she was right.

He was our salvation right from the beginning. He was always there for me, telling me things would be alright. I knew he'd felt helpless watching her broken little soul suffering such pain, but he'd handled it differently. As a mother, I worried endlessly and my anxiety showed. It was difficult for me to resist asking those typical motherly questions every time I saw her: "How are you feeling? Do you need anything? What can I do?" It drove her crazy. Stuart was way more patient than me, and knew how to simply be there for Sophie. He was the strong, steady presence, picking her up when she faltered, listening when she needed an ear and constantly encouraging her to keep moving forward. He knew how to give unconditional love and I was overjoyed Sophie recognised it too. It was an important step on Sophie's road to recovery, but the hardest ones were still to come.

Chapter 7
Secrets

When Dr Rama called me late one afternoon I hoped it would be with good news, but it wasn't. Sophie's father had ignored her advice and was trying to contact Sophie at the clinic, not once but many times. "Rose, I want you to go to the police and request an intervention order. Explain the situation and give them my details so they can contact me."

This was more serious than I thought. I acted immediately, reporting the situation to the local police and setting the wheels in motion. I discovered he had somehow accessed an app on Sophie's phone and deleted some of his own messages. He also tried to have Sophie transferred back to the city where he lived, and even had the audacity to register her with a school up there. My conversation with Stuart that evening was very confronting. Usually we talked about Sophie's progress and he would reassure me everything would work out, then I would try to compart-mentalise my fears so I could function for another day. We never went out and only my closest friends knew what was happening. But now

Stuart voiced what I couldn't bear to think. "Could he have inappropriately touched her?"

"God no!" But my hasty denial didn't reflect what I felt when he asked that question. I had asked myself the same thing a million times over the last few weeks. Something dreadful must be at the root of Sophie's pain, and Dr Rama's concerns were like a big signpost pointing to her father.

Despite that, I couldn't grasp how the man I was married to for so long could be capable of hurting his children. "There is no doubt he is a sick bastard and he loathes me, but the children? He would never do anything like that to them." Even as the words passed my lips, the question circled back through my mind; *but could he?* If the past had taught me anything, it's that secrets can be hidden for a terribly long time.

~

Sophie maintained a stubborn silence about anything to do with her therapy. She was still on medication and it stole the light from her eyes. In the mirror, my own eyes looked similar, haunted by doubt and uncertainty. I'd experienced periods of both sharp pain and dull pain in my life, and there would be more of both to come, but these few weeks were a lonely sort of pain. My mind made up so many stories about what might have happened but I rarely voiced them, even to Stuart who I knew would have helped me cope. Instead I dwelled too much on all the worst possibilities until I felt trapped in a deep, dark well with not a sliver of light to show me the way out.

Why didn't I ask Sophie and relieve myself of the distress? Because I didn't have the right to ease my own pain at the expense of causing more to someone else, particularly my daughter. Forcing her to talk about something she hadn't yet chosen to share with me felt selfish. I had to let her come to it in her own time, or accept the possibility that she may never wish to do so. Sometimes we must have blind faith in the ones we love. We must support them when they need us, even if we don't know why. My belief in Sophie wasn't dependent on knowing what she knew. It wasn't dependent on anything. Unconditional love is simply that – without limit or expectations. And if a mother cannot show this type of love to her child, who will?

Standing by someone when you don't know what happened or why they are hurting, brings its own challenges. I had to bury my ego and resist my natural urge to take control of the situation. I had to manage my frustration when little steps forward were followed by sharp slides back. I'm a natural fixer, diving fast into problems and driving hard towards a solution, but I had to put my faith in the relationship between Sophie and the medical professionals at the clinic. I hoped it was the right place for her secrets to be revealed and healed. What Sophie needed from me was all the stuff I find hardest to do: waiting patiently, letting her find her own way, quietly being there. It was so difficult.

I struggled to get through each day. My attention span was short and my energy scarce. If I could ignore something, I did. Anything I could jettison was gone. Life became a robotic routine that got me from my bed, to my office, to Sophie's bedside and back home. I went shopping only for essentials, I kept cancelling my haircuts, all exercise ceased and friendships were on hold.

My job was demanding. A team of three managers relied on me to make decisions and be their leader. My boss, who was so supportive in the beginning, eventually put more pressure on the team and on me. She had no choice. The board demanded results, and I was determined not to let my team down. As their leader, it was my role to inspire them, relieve them of obstacles and keep my eye on the big picture. While I felt overwhelmed and exhausted most days, we managed to hit our targets, mainly due to their hard work and willingness to take on extra responsibilities. They were a wonderful team. I was also blessed with the most amazing assistant, a very organised person who I could count on to keep things together for me. The thing I loved most was her incredibly sincere and caring nature. She was one in a million, covering for me many times when life became increasingly complex.

~

A few weeks later, Stuart convinced me it was time to tell my parents. I'd been putting that off, but it was becoming difficult to hide that something was going on. My father suffered from a heart condition and I didn't want to cause him more stress, but to be honest it was my mother's reaction I was avoiding. I knew she would make me feel I had somehow caused this. She might not say as much but it would be there, a palpable censure. I couldn't deal with that right now. She loved Sophie and my other children unconditionally, as grandmothers often do. It seemed her disapproval was reserved for me.

Stuart made the call to my father, knowing I couldn't face one more emotional conversation. They were shocked and insisted they would make the trip to be with us for the intervention order court hearing, which was scheduled to take place one month later. My mother was not well. She hadn't been able to walk for five years and was confined to a motorised scooter. Dad was her constant carer and I was concerned about them travelling. But Dad had told me several times that they found it more stressful when I shut them out, trying to protect them from what was going on in my life. The thing is, it wasn't only them I was trying to protect. My mother's love never felt unconditional, and my natural-born forthrightness made me an easy victim of her skilled manipulation.

My mother thrived on drama, and if there wasn't any, she created it. She particularly enjoyed playing family members off against each other. When I discovered my husband's sick lifestyle, I knew if I revealed the full story to my parents it would be irresistible fuel for her trouble-making ways. The shame I felt upon learning of the deception in my marriage would be magnified by my mother somehow, someway. I couldn't bear the thought of dealing with her when I was already at my lowest, and

I didn't want my children to discover the horrid revelation through some overcooked family spectacle, so I only told my parents that he was meeting up with people online, keeping the worst details secret. When I broached the possibility of leaving him, my mother told me it wasn't a good enough reason. "You'll regret breaking your family up over this. Sometimes you have to look past your own feelings and do what's right for the family," she warned.

I knew my mother had fallen for my husband's charisma from the day she met him. Maybe she recognised a fellow manipulator, an ally, but also a competitor to join her game of family control. Was it my youth, or maybe my naivety that blinded me to these signs of danger? They say girls marry men like their father, but I married a man like my mother. The poisonous seeds of doubt she planted early in my life by always finding fault, grew into a tangle of weeds during my years of marriage to a master manipulator, and they began to strangle me.

I summoned enough courage to refuse his efforts to return to the family home after that fateful Easter holiday, but my courage dissolved within weeks after my parents invited him to stay in their guest house. I felt betrayed on all sides and had no energy to fight their united pressure. Against my better judgement, I let him return to the family home. We didn't break up until three years later, and they were the worst years of my life. Until now.

Chapter 8
Coming Home

Two weeks after arriving at the clinic, Dr Rama felt confident to plan Sophie's return home. It was important for her to experience some normality, she explained, but it was also crucial for Sophie to continue receiving strong support. She would need to remain on medication, which Dr Rama would monitor weekly, and also undertake weekly sessions with a psychologist so she could begin proper therapy for her trauma. She warned us not to assume this meant Sophie was 'better'; it simply meant she was no longer an immediate danger to herself. She was stable enough to continue her therapy while returning to school and reconnecting with her normal life.

I was excited at the prospect of having Sophie home, but petrified at the same time. A few days before she was due to be discharged, I pulled my car into the garage after an exhausting day at work and found Stuart in the kitchen ready to serve up dinner. Moving in to steal a kiss and wrap those big arms around me, he asked how my day was.

"Work was hectic as always and Sophie, well, she seems to be thinking a lot about coming home."

"How does it make you feel?" he asked.

"Very anxious. I don't know if she is ready, or more to the point, I don't know if *I'm* ready. What happens if she gets seriously low again? How are we going to handle it? I must admit, I'm scared."

"Well, I've been thinking about it," he said. "Her birthday is coming up and it's a well-known fact that dogs, especially labradors, are great therapy. I think we should consider getting her a dog."

"Yes!" I cried, seizing the idea like a drowning woman desperately grasping a lifeline. Somewhere along the way I'd become obsessed with the idea I should be able to fix Sophie. I felt it was my job to find the 'something' that would fix everything. So far I'd been treading water, unable to gain a foothold in the sands shifting beneath my feet. I felt useless and it was exhausting. I'm a person who believes every problem has a solution, and I'm happiest when I can see an immediate result for my efforts. When I don't, I double down and try harder. It makes me impetuous but also determined. I can't easily be swayed once I've seized an idea. I'd been struggling to find something to revive Sophie's spark and Stuart's idea sounded perfect. Surely a cute, dependent little puppy would give her something to live for?

Before the dinner plates even reached the table, I'd begun searching the internet for breeders. I scrolled and scrolled through pages of puppies until I found a litter of the most adorable labradors. Without hesitation, I picked up the phone and called the breeder. The woman confirmed she had two left and they would be available in the next week.

I couldn't wait to tell Sophie the great news. Armed with puppy photos, I raced out of work at lunchtime the next day and straight to the clinic. Sophie seemed to be in much better spirits than usual. I gave her the biggest hug and launched straight into the big sales pitch: "You know how you've always wanted your own dog?" She nodded slowly and tilted her head as she waited to hear where this was heading. "Well, Dad and I thought it would be a great idea if we got you a puppy."

"Really? I can have my very own puppy?" She bounced on the bed, hands clasped at her chin and her face suddenly beaming.

"Yes, of course. I've already done some research and found the most gorgeous labrador pups." I handed her my phone and nestled up close while she scrolled through the photos. I revelled in her child-like excitement, something I'd not seen in such a long time. "Mum, I love this one." She was pointing to the smallest puppy, a ball of velvety fur with big brown eyes. "When can we get him?"

"They won't be ready for a week, so if you continue to do really well and the doctor confirms you can come home, we can go together and collect him." It gave her something to look forward to, and most importantly, something to work towards. Staring into the puppy's captivating eyes, she said, "I can't wait to tell Dr Rama when she comes this afternoon."

This is the answer, I thought. *It could fix everything.*

⌒‿

We were all excited by the idea of having a new puppy and I was no longer apprehensive about bringing Sophie home. She settled back into daily life surprisingly easily, and our first order of business was to head to a pet store to buy everything we needed for the gorgeous little bundle who was about to become part of our family. We loaded our arms high with all possible doggy essentials (and lots of non-essentials) and exited the store with a much lighter bank balance. But it was worth every cent to see Sophie full of anticipation and smiling more than she had for months.

A few days later, we woke early to make the two-and-a-half-hour trip to the breeder. I hadn't been outside the city for a long time and I could feel myself relax as the buildings slowly faded in the rear-view mirror. The cool autumn day rewarded us with a clear blue sky, and it was delicious to travel along empty roads through lush, green countryside. When we arrived at our destination I took a moment to breathe in the fresh air and listen to the peaceful rustle of leaves in the big oak trees surrounding the breeder's property.

A lady appeared with two young children in tow. They welcomed us into the large yard and led us to a pen where puppies were bouncing in playful circles and climbing over each other. It was the sort of distracting entertainment we could have watched all day, but the youngest girl reached in and pulled Sophie's puppy out of the throng. She handed him over and Sophie wrapped him in her arms, rubbing her face against his soft fur. "Mum, this is Buddy," she introduced us. "Isn't he so cute?"

Buddy became her shadow in no time at all. He followed her, slept with her, even showered with her. The house was alive with puppy love and we all began to relax a little. Sophie went back to school and I went to work without the added pressure of rushing to the clinic every lunchtime and evening. But the normality was fleeting. Slowly, almost imperceptibly, Sophie withdrew. She spent more time in her room, and when she was with us she would quickly become irritable and negative. Then she began skipping school, struggling to get out of bed at all. Her smile faded and her eyes became haunted. I tried to work from home, nervous about leaving her alone. On the days when she was low, Buddy would sense it and stay faithfully by her side. But whatever was going on inside, the pain was greater than her love for little Buddy and his adoration of her.

☙

One morning before breakfast I tapped on Sophie's bedroom door as usual. There was no response. I pushed the door ajar but the room was empty. As I turned to leave, my eye caught a glimpse of something scarlet on her bed. *Oh no, there's blood on her sheets.* Racing straight into her

61

bathroom, I found Sophie sitting on the edge of the bath, crying uncontrollably and bleeding from the gashes she'd hacked into her thighs.

I screamed out to Stuart and he came running up the stairs as I wrapped my arms around her and manoeuvred her onto the floor. I held her gently, sobbing with her while Stuart checked her injuries.

He cleaned away the blood and said, "Sophie, we need to take you to a hospital. The cuts are so deep, you need stiches."

"Please, Dad, don't take me there, I'm begging you. If you take me there I won't come out."

"Honey, we have to do something. It's not safe."

"Dad, please don't. I promise I won't do it again."

"Look, I've got some surgical strips here. We can try to close the wounds with them. But the three of us need to come up with a strategy to help you." Stuart carefully applied the strips, doing his best to close the cuts, then he bandaged the tops of her legs. I was too terrified to let her go and continued holding her body against mine.

When Stuart finished, he sat back and asked, "What did you use?"

She looked over to the shower. "I found one of Mum's razor blades."

How could I be so stupid? I should have known better.

"I've got an idea," said Stuart, and he disappeared down the stairs. When he returned he held two rubber bands. "I've been doing some research." He put the rubber bands on Sophie's wrist. "Every time you feel the urge to cut yourself, snap the bands on your wrist very hard so they hurt. It means you'll feel pain, but won't do any damage. Do you think you can do this? No, actually, can you *promise* me you will do it?"

Sophie had no choice but to agree, otherwise she knew he would take her straight back to the clinic.

~

While some professionals might suggest self-harm is not a sign of suicidal tendencies, Dr Rama advised us that those who self-harm are at an increased risk of making an attempt on their life. For Sophie, this proved to be the case. It was clear she was battling overwhelming emotions and didn't know how to handle whatever what going on inside. Self-harm was an attempt to gain relief from emotional pain by inflicting physical pain instead, but it simply left Sophie in more distress. We discovered that Sophie's first self-harm episode occurred before she came to live with us, but we knew little of what triggered it. All we could do now was remain alert and try to avert the risk before she felt as if her only option was to hurt herself.

Sophie would always cut in the shower. For some reason it was where she had panic attacks. One time she hit her fist on the tiles so hard she bruised all her knuckles. Once I was aware of the pattern, I tried to always be nearby while she showered. Even if I couldn't be there, Stuart would sit out of sight, talking with her and trying to put her at ease so she could shower safely. I was reminded of the many times when, as a little girl, she wouldn't shower unless I went into the bathroom with her. I wish I'd been wiser to those signs back then.

〜

The nightmare had returned and I was haunted by visions of losing Sophie. We were once again walking on eggshells, and I was back sleeping on the floor outside her bedroom door. Within a week Sophie cut herself with a pair of old scissors, reopening her unhealed wounds. While Stuart focused on stemming the blood, I phoned Dr Rama's mobile number. She was at home with her family but told us to bring Sophie straight to the clinic, where she would meet us. This time Sophie didn't refuse.

"Apparently her father has been trying to contact her," Dr Rama explained when she came to see us in the waiting room after speaking with Sophie. "When she didn't respond, he cut off her phone." It was the only thing he'd been paying for, and this was exactly the sort of controlling thing he would do. She'd borne it all in a silent struggle of conflicting emotions that must have been so confusing for her vulnerable young mind. I was livid at his callous disregard for her mental state and for ignoring the interim intervention order. The court hearing was just around the corner and it couldn't come soon enough as far as I was concerned.

Stuart immediately went to the store and bought Sophie a new phone. She remained in the clinic for three days. Even though her homecoming was more subdued this time, I somehow felt more ready. Sophie's relapse was a reality check for me. It dawned on me that there could be no shortcuts in the struggle to heal the mental anguish consuming her. There is no quick fix. Finding a way back from the edge of a cliff is a raw and tortuous expedition requiring more courage, patience and persistence than I could ever have imagined, not only from Sophie, but from anyone who loved her and wanted to help her. Rather than expecting life to return to normal, I prepared myself for the long haul. The anxiety felt more familiar, and I slipped back into my routine of watchfulness, sharing my regular patrols up to Sophie's room with the ever-present Buddy, who was never far from her side.

Chapter 9
Revelations

A few days before the intervention order court hearing, Dr Rama emailed me a letter she had sent to the police and asked me to take it the hearing. I opened it, but as my eyes scanned the content my heart stopped. I stared at just one sentence, trying desperately to comprehend the words; "She has a childhood history of trauma due to sexual abuse."

My body trembled uncontrollably. Suddenly I was sweating, then a wave of nausea gripped my stomach. With no time to reach the bathroom, I grabbed the bin beside my desk and vomited violently. My heart was thumping so hard I thought it would surely explode. I felt faint, aware of only one thing – the voice in my head moaning over and over, *Nooo …*

This shock was different to the night when I was woken by Sophie with blood on her shirt. Then I was filled with terror and panic, and yes, my body was racked with heart-pounding tremors, but I had woken ignorant to the fateful shifts about to befall my family. In a matter of weeks, the story of my life, or at least the version I carried around in my memory, had been shredded into small pieces and scattered to oblivion by a relentless storm. I'd been forced to watch a new story emerge, scrawled by the desperate actions of my daughter and punctuated by words I didn't want to hear. How many times had I approached the possibility that the cause of Sophie's pain was something so evil? And just as many times, I'd backed away. I hid in the shadows of doubt, letting their dark folds protect me from the undeniable truth that my child had been abused. But with those unambiguous and clinical words, my shelter was swept away and my deepest dread exposed.

I clutched the phone, unable to think of anything except to reach Stuart. I was desperate to hear the voice that calmed me, gave me hope and loved me no matter what. My hands were shaking hard and I couldn't even hold my thumb in place long enough to open the damn thing. I quickly gave up and tapped in my passcode instead. As the phone rang, I paced up and down the lounge room.

"Rosey," he answered warmly. The moment he answered I stopped pacing, but the words wouldn't come. They were stuck at the back of my throat, held there by what felt like a dam wall about to crack.

"Rose ... what's the matter?" Stuart implored. That was all it took for the dam to break. Hysterical sobs, gasping breaths and half-formed words tumbled over each other as I collapsed down to the ground. Nothing made sense and I knew it.

"Rose, please, slow down and breathe with me." I let his words soothe me, "In – two three ... out – two three."

He continued for some time and I followed his rhythm until my breath and my heart slowed down. By then Stuart was pulling into our driveway, and I dropped the phone and ran outside. I launched myself into his arms, sobbing anew as I buried my face in his chest. Finally I was able to utter the words, "She has been sexually abused."

He wrapped his arms more tightly around me and we stood there in a long embrace. I didn't want to let go.

The house was quiet. It was late, but sleep eluded me. I turned my head to look at Stuart's face cradled gently in his pillow. He looked so relaxed and his breath was soft and rhythmic. I knew Sophie would be lost in the drug-induced sleep designed to 'protect' her. I slid out of bed and crept silently through the dark house to the back door. It led straight into the garage, and as I closed the door behind me, I flicked on the light. My car was pushed up against the wall and there was just enough space for me to sidle around in front of it. I looked up at the shelves beside the workbench. They were full of the usual garage stuff: bottles of car oil, a bucket, a hose, a few gardening tools and small boxes filled with odd screws and nails. I found what I was looking for tucked into the lower shelves.

The boxes had moved with me from house to house, remaining unopened for almost four years. I hauled the first one out and lifted it onto the bench. Slicing through the ragged old tape with a nail, I pushed open the four stiff cardboard folds and knew instantly it was the one I had been seeking. It was full of photo albums, a chronicle of family life I hadn't looked at for many years. I knew which one held Sophie's baby photos and I lifted it out, laying it gently on the bench. I peeled open the hard cover, and the faded little pictures of Sophie's tiny face swaddled in a white wrap transported me back to the day of her birth. Being my youngest, I wasn't too worried when I felt contractions during the afternoon, but I knew this would be the day. We were fishing with the kids and I wanted to get them home, fed, bathed and in bed before heading to the hospital. Maybe Sophie was already flagging her readiness to fit into our crazy family schedule, because I achieved it all and arrived at the hospital around 7pm. But she didn't wait much longer. Even as I repeated my request for an epidural for the fourth time, making it clear to the midwife that yes, I was *sure* I wanted one, Sophie decided she would wait no longer. Three hours after leaving home my perfect little girl was in my arms.

I continued turning the pages of the album. There was a photo of me looking lovingly into her face, lost in the wonder of a whole new human who had just been placed in my arms and entrusted to my care. My helpless little baby. I was supposed to protect her. Tears threatened to blind me but I swept them roughly aside with the back of my hand. The letter didn't say who abused her and Dr Rama would not tell me. I couldn't ask Sophie. She was still too close to the edge. *How did this happen? When did it happen? Who did this to my daughter? Was it her father?* Everything pointed to him but I needed to know for sure.

I searched the photos in the album looking for a sign, hoping for an answer to appear before my eyes. As I turned the pages, her fine little features took form, revealing that sweet familiar smile framed by dimples. There she was in the arms of her sister. On the next page she was lying on a rug while her brother played with his trucks around her. And there we were as a family at her christening. I studied her face in every photo. What had I missed?

From an early age, Sophie was an anxious child, always clinging to me and not wanting to be apart. She was often afraid of men, but she was a shy little girl and I didn't think her timidity was strange at the time. My thoughts went to the local social get-togethers, neighbours gathered around the barbeque laughing while the kids played nearby. I recalled how some of the men, Sophie's father included, made crude jokes with each other and teased the kids. Even though Sophie was so young, not even in school, simply witnessing such interactions was enough to make her run to me in tears. Holding her tight, I could feel her tiny body tremble. It was cruel.

Most nights when she went to bed, I would have to lie beside her. I loved doing this because we led such busy lives and it became my special time with her at the end of the day. We would chat, read a story, sing a song together or just cuddle until she settled. I hadn't read anything into it, just like her resistance to showering alone.

She often had stomach troubles, constantly complaining of tummy pains. Over the years we visited doctors, dieticians and naturopaths many times over. We tried different therapies and eliminated various foods from her diet, but nothing worked. Only six months earlier we'd been referred to a new gastroenterologist who asked her to swallow a small camera in a capsule to see what was going on – still nothing.

When puberty arrived, Sophie had dreadful problems and showed signs of early endometriosis. Only in the last few years has medical research identified an apparent link between endometriosis and child sexual abuse, due to the damage it can cause to the structure around the uterus. It was one more sign we didn't understand at the time. She was also a bedwetter when young, and frequently had thrush. I was so concerned about it at one stage, I even asked my mum if it was normal. I remember my mother asking me if there was any way Sophie's father could be touching her inappropriately. I was so offended and upset; how could she even suggest my husband, the father of these innocent young children, could ever do something like that. Yes, there were sick people out there in the world, but not in *my* family.

What hellish regret I suffered, and it still rears its head in unexpected moments. Why did I so carelessly brush aside these signs? Was I so lost in my busy family and work life that I'd rushed straight past something so important? Was I too focused on the pain of my warped marriage to notice the hurt and distress of my child? I should have seen something. I should have known. Discovering my daughter suffered while I did nothing was impossible to bear. Regret eats at your soul like a malignant cancer, and it buried itself deep in my cells. The revelation of such a secret became a lightning rod for all the moments of regret in my life. Before this, I'd tolerated wrongs done to me in silence, keeping secrets in the mistaken belief I was protecting my children. Discovering my daughter had been wronged made me wish I could go back and change it all. But I still didn't know for sure what needed to be changed …

Behind the big wooden door lay a courtroom. I'd never been inside one for real, but I'd seen plenty of them in movies and the reality matched the fiction. Stuart, Dad and I arrived early for the intervention order (IVO) hearing and were greeted by the same sort of security we were accustomed to navigating at airports. I placed my handbag onto a tray and the guys emptied their pockets before we passed one by one through the beeping portal to another world.

It was not necessary for Sophie to appear, and I was relieved she would not be exposed to this situation. If I thought the medical world was mysterious, the legal world would prove even more difficult to comprehend; again the impersonal corridors, security cameras and endless waiting. I wasn't quite sure what we were waiting for as we sat side by side on seats lining the corridor outside one of the courtrooms. Stuart and Dad both wore suits and I was dressed in one of my better business outfits, but when I looked around at the other people waiting on the hard plastic seats, I felt a little overdressed. We were a broad cross-section of society, strangers sharing the same space for a moment as we lived through our own private dramas. Each of us waited to be judged or defended, prosecuted or protected.

I was anxious whether Sophie's father would be there. Every time someone new turned the corner I looked up, but deep down I knew he would never part with the money to fly in. Eventually a man appeared in front of me and introduced himself as the police prosecutor who would be representing Sophie. "Rose, we are going to ask for an intervention order of three years. The magistrate usually only grants one year, but given the situation, we are optimistic." I nodded, still overwhelmed by the new environment.

The courtroom doors opened a few moments later and the gathered crowd moved forward to claim seats in the public area facing the judge's bench. Dad sat on one side of me and Stuart on the other, my protectors, my rocks. The magistrate entered from a side door and we all stood. I caught a glimpse of a black gown moving towards the high bench before us, but it wasn't until everyone sat down that I saw her. Because she was wearing the loose robe of a judge, it was her face that drew my eye. She looked stern and serious, but also sincere.

We were the first case on the morning schedule. My heart raced as I listened to the prosecutor outline the details. He handed over a file to the clerk, who passed it to the magistrate. She sat silent for a few moments scanning the document then, with a dramatic flick of her head and a tone worthy of a stage performance, she spoke: "I have a written response from the other party saying he cannot make the hearing on such short notice, or afford the expense of travelling here. He advises he will not be contesting the IVO on condition his terms are met. He demands the order to be in place for only one year, the mother to keep him up-to-date on the child with regular reports, and the treating doctor to also provide him with regular updates." My relief at his non-appearance evaporated as I listened to the list of conditions. Even from a distance he was trying to control us, but the magistrate put down the folder and her voice rose sharply; "I don't know who on earth he thinks he is, but he will not demand anything from the courts."

Relief rushed back. In fact, I felt almost euphoric. Wow, she could see through him. I wanted to hug her right then and there. She quickly continued; "I understand the child cannot be here today. Is anyone here on her behalf?"

"Yes, the mother is here," the prosecutor pointed in my direction.

I felt all eyes in the room fix on me as I stood. "It's fine, you can remain seated," said the magistrate. My face flushed red with embarrassment as I sat back down. So, not everything was like the movies.

"Does the other party have a job?" she asked.

"Yes, Your Honour." I replied

"Does he pay the required child support?"

"No, Your Honour."

"That doesn't surprise me." She looked back at the folder then over to the prosecutor. "Prosecution, does he have a criminal record?"

"Yes he does, Your Honour."

What? The sudden jolt of my head must have been noticeable. I didn't know that. Who the hell *is* this man I was married to for all those years? How and when did he get a criminal record?

The magistrate turned back to me. "I have read through the psychiatrist's letter. It is very disturbing. Were you aware of the sexual abuse?"

"No, Your Honour, not until we received the letter." With that, all attempts to hold myself together failed. Tears rolled down my cheeks.

Her voice softened. "Is your daughter safe and are you safe?"

"Yes, Your Honour. We are doing everything we can to keep her safe."

"The safety of you and your daughter is the court's priority. I see here the police are requesting an IVO be put in place for three years."

My heart sank, anticipating she might only grant the order for one year. I hoped we could get two years, by which time Sophie would be eighteen and in a better position to decide for herself what she felt was best. After all, this was about Sophie having the opportunity to take back control of her life.

"I note you are not formally on the request for the order. I am going to add you to it and grant the intervention order for five years. Do you think that is sufficient?"

"Yes, Your Honour," I responded with surprise.

"No, actually I think it should be ten," she said triumphantly. "What do you think of ten years?" she asked, looking at me with a steely but concerned gaze.

Shocked, I didn't know what to say. I felt immense gratitude for the sense of security and validation she had already provided, but I've always been cautious about drawing my children into the bitter conflict between their parents. While it was tempting to agree to ten years, I didn't want to make a decision quite this significant on Sophie's behalf.

"Your Honour, if we could please do five years, by then I am hopeful Sophie will be much healthier and stronger, and she can decide what she would prefer to do about her father."

"Alright, we will make it for five years. Prosecution, I'm adding the mother to the order as well. Are you in agreeance?"

"Yes, Your Honour."

As we left the courthouse I felt we'd taken another big step on the path to Sophie's recovery. Later, when I told her about the hearing and handed her the intervention order, I could sense Sophie's relief too. Standing at the door to her room, I watched her remove a photo from one of the frames near her bed and insert the court document in its place. She put it right in the middle of her dressing table and turned to me with a serene face; "That's protecting me."

～

The hearing unearthed another confusing puzzle – the criminal record. I asked Stuart and Dad if they heard what I heard and they both said, "Yes." I couldn't understand how it was possible. He was in the military when we married, and he couldn't have a criminal record while serving. Then I remembered the odd way his military career ended. Normally he would be required to give twelve months notice if he wanted to get out, but before Sophie was born, when we were only eight months into a posting in a major city, he came home one day and told me he was to be discharged. He'd been on shiftwork; an unpredictable schedule which left me much like a single mother with very young children. He said he thought it would be best for me and the children if he ended his military career, and he'd received special consideration for it to happen immediately. I was surprised, but also excited at the thought of being back near family and friends, so I never thought to question it. During the month we waited for the discharge to be finalized, he was taken off shiftwork and put back on normal hours. I was happy to have him around the house for the final month while we packed up and prepared for the last of our four moves in only five years, but the sudden change to his situation and all the inconsistencies in his story made me wonder if there was more to it.

Years later, my business won a contract with a government agency, subject to criminal checks. He was knocked back. He told me they had mixed him up with another person of the same name. Again, I never questioned it. I was so naive. Was everything in our marriage a lie?

Chapter 10
The Bridge

Moving around the country as a military wife can be a lonely life, but I was grateful for one thing – the people who befriended me. Macy and Tim were a couple who took me under their wing during those years, and they'd remained firm friends ever since. When Sophie was born I asked them to be her godparents and they took on the role with great enthusiasm. Even though we lived in different cities by then, they would always make the effort to be present for important events in her life, and Macy was one of the first people I confided in a few weeks after we rushed Sophie to hospital the first time.

With the IVO hearing behind us, we needed a change of scenery, so we decided to visit Macy and Tim for a long weekend. They lived in the nation's capital, about seven hours drive from us. Being new puppy parents, we'd forgotten to factor in Buddy's doggy do-do stops, so the trip stretched out to eight and a half hours. It was nice to be away from the city, watching the expansive countryside slip past the window and taking short Buddy walks between the trees at our roadside stops.

Our first night with such close friends was a welcome escape from what had become our harsh reality. Stuart and I had avoided going out for any social occasion in the last six weeks, but here I felt comfortable. I could laugh and joke, or share my saddest moments, and I knew they would understand what I needed.

Macy was caring for a friend's horses that weekend and Sophie eagerly volunteered to help feed them. Sophie had her own horse before our family life disintegrated, and, at thirteen, she'd taken it hard when she learned she'd have to give him up. When they returned, I could see Macy was angling for some alone time with me so we grabbed a glass of wine and wandered into the backyard. "I had a bit of a chat with Sophie," she said. "I told her it's important for her to let you in and tell you whatever is going on." I was grateful Macy had the sort of relationship with Sophie that allowed her to raise what I could not. "I hope it helps," she finished.

The car was quiet as we travelled the long road home after our few days with these great friends. It wasn't an uncomfortable silence. In fact the tension accompanying us in recent weeks might have dissolved a little. Maybe it had been good for Sophie to spend time with other people.

⌒

Being a friend to someone who is enduring tough times is not easy. Friends want to help, but sometimes their version of help … well, it doesn't really help. It takes a fair degree of sensitivity to know when someone needs to talk about their dramas, and when they need the distraction of light and friendly banter. I didn't want Sophie's life to become someone else's circus show, so I confided in few people. It was easier to avoid probing questions than feel obliged to keep people updated. I wasn't very good at setting boundaries, and it took me some time to learn how to say, "I'm not in a space to talk about it now."

We also didn't encourage Sophie to get too close to anyone she met during her stays at the clinic. As a teenager, the potential to be influenced by other young people was a risk Dr Rama urged us to monitor closely. There's a fine line between being inspired by others, and being swayed by them. It's not that I don't believe in the importance of asking for help and letting people in, but it was clear Sophie needed professional help at that point in her journey.

⌒

A week later, on a day when Sophie was clearly feeling very low, I bundled her into the car for one of her appointments. She was crying constantly, and angry at me for dragging her out of the house. On our way back home, I tried to say encouraging things about her efforts and how I believed she would get well and have a better life. It was a one-sided conversation, and I should have remained quiet that day, but I was always trying a little too hard to make things better.

The traffic was thick as we skirted the edge of the city right on 5pm. Our most direct route home was via the fast-moving, five-laned motorway across one of the busiest bridges in town. Just as I was speeding up to merge into a slight gap between the racing cars, I asked, "How are you feeling?"

Sophie's sadness turned unexpectedly to rage. "How do you think I feel?" she screamed. "You sit there trying to *fix* me and you have no idea! How would you feel if your own father forced himself in you?"

A sickening wave of shock surged through my body. My hands froze on the steering wheel and for a moment everything went grey. Only pure survival instinct saved us from crashing. The sound of blaring horns woke me from my daze and I became aware of blurred colours as cars whizzed past on either side.

"What do you mean? What are you saying?!" I blurted.

"I don't want to talk about it," she snapped.

My mind was blank. I couldn't have said anything else even if I tried. All I could hear was my ragged breath echoing in my head. I steered the car off at the next exit with trembling hands and drove slowly through the last few streets to our house.

Back home with Sophie safely in her room, I too retreated to my bedroom. Stuart hadn't arrived home yet and I felt my emotions churn like a pot about to boil over. Her abuser *was* her father – the man I had chosen to love and marry, to raise a family with, who stood beside me at their school concerts, sat amongst us at the dinner table, lit the candles on their birthday cakes, carried their sleepy bodies up to bed at night.

I couldn't comprehend how anyone could do something so horrid. You think the people you let into your life have similar values and similar limits. While I'd gradually recognised there was a huge chasm between his values and mine on so many levels, in my wildest dreams I never pictured this. But I didn't doubt Sophie for one moment. She never gave me any reason to disbelieve her. I was still in the dark about when, where and how it had taken place, but now I knew who had perpetrated such cruelty to an innocent child. Knowing this sharpened my guilt. I kept reliving the past, trying to work out where I went wrong. Looking through new eyes, I could see signs everywhere. *Why didn't I notice? Why hadn't I done something? Why couldn't I just go back and change things?*

Muffling my sobs in my pillow, I let the enormity of my daughter's tragic revelation hit me. There was no more doubt, no ambiguity to hide behind, and no reason to hold back my burning hatred and rage. I couldn't stop the violent mix of thoughts and feelings from rising. I imagined the many slow and painful ways I could end his life or make him suffer the sort of agony he had inflicted on my daughter. I didn't realise how much I could hate someone, and these vengeful thoughts scared me. The fantasy of wreaking revenge is a horrifying mind game. If I could think such vicious things, I wondered what made me any different to him or the multitude of cruel people who believe they have some right to dominate others? But I knew the answer. I could never do it. The idea of inflicting injury or pain on another person repulses me. A bitter fantasy of revenge could never make me cross that line.

Chapter 11
Loss

Stuart was the most amazing father. He never wavered in his support for Sophie and he showed her nothing but unconditional love. He was always trying to think of practical ways to convince her she was the most amazing, beautiful soul.

Several years earlier he'd tattooed the names and birth years of both his sons on his right arm. He always said he would never get a woman's name tattooed on him, but he decided he wanted to add Sophie. It was his way of proving he was never going to leave her. She was initially sceptical when he excitedly shared his plan, but we had learnt not to let her low moods derail us. Within a week Stuart and Sophie were at the tattoo parlour getting her name permanently on his arm.

I was in the shower when they came barging into the ensuite. Stuart proudly showed me his arm covered in plastic wrap, and I could faintly see the outline of her name. But there was something else. Right above Sophie's name was mine, the familiar *Rosey*. I was speechless, astonished that Stuart would permanently put my name on his arm. Then he boldly declared, "Both you girls are stuck with me now." Sophie stood there beaming, her gorgeous dimples framing the wide smile I hadn't seen in a very long time.

~

It was not only the abuse inflicted by her biological father that Sophie was working through, it was also the rejection. Her sense of self-worth was incredibly low. She was a kind, smart and sassy girl with endless potential. When she was young, she loved science and wanted to be a doctor or a nurse – anything to help other people – but she no longer had any dreams for her future. Our treasured girl no longer treasured herself.

Stuart went to great lengths to show her how much he treasured her. He'd stepped easily into the role of loving father, and he told her often, "Honey, I choose you because I see the beautiful and magical soul you are." But they were only words. Actions speak louder and Stuart was a man of action. Some of his ideas worked and some of them didn't. Sometimes Sophie would try them and sometimes she wouldn't. After participating in a few self-defence lessons, she decided it wasn't for her, but she enjoyed going to the gym and training with him. Getting her out the door for anything was a struggle, and even though she enjoyed the gym, it was no different. You could see the battle going on in her mind each morning – the tiny flame of desire to be engaged in some-thing uplifting vs. the lethargy of depression that depleted her willpower. Often the lethargy won, but on the days when she hauled herself out of bed, she would return from the gym brighter and more positive. It was a fitting reward for the enormous effort it took for her to achieve anything these days.

One Sunday morning Stuart arranged to take Sophie shopping for a Dad and Daughter ring. They headed out in the drizzling rain and I looked forward to pottering at home, a rare and much-needed break by myself. It was a cold winter morning, only four months since my waking nightmare had begun. In some ways it felt like years had passed, but I was still struggling to find any sort of routine. The one constant in this new existence was my anxiety. I was in a persistent state of vigilance, watchful for any slight indication that Sophie was struggling more than usual. Relaxing felt uncomfortable, even when I knew she was in safe hands. So when my phone rang and I saw it was my dad's familiar number, I was happy for the distraction. "Hey, Dad," I answered lightly.

"Rose, darling," he replied in a shaky voice. "Your mother just passed away."

~~~

It was nearly two months since they had visited us. After a lifetime of emotional battles, my mother and I made peace during that visit. I'd tried many times before to engage her in a serious conversation about our relationship, but she'd always found a way to avoid it. She would look me up and down, clearly assessing me against some inner standard, and I always came up short. "Rose, you must do something about your hair," or, "No, no, no, the colour is all wrong on you," or the simplest of put-downs, "You look fat in that dress."

My mother had a strange upbringing. Adopted by an older couple who lived a very straitlaced Victorian life, she was the odd child dressed in stockings and pinafores when the other kids wore shorts and runners. The pressure to meet a standard from another era surely clipped my mother's wings and tamed her spirit. She cruelly discovered she was adopted when told by some kids at school, and her eventual reunion with her birth mother was no fairytale. Despite it all, my father recalls the vivacious woman he met when she was studying to be a nurse. She was outgoing, a free spirit who everyone wanted to befriend.

In her second year of studies, while on holidays with friends, she had a bad waterskiing accident, breaking her pelvis and injuring her back.

This one moment changed her life, leaving her in with a degenerative spine and in constant pain. It was the 1960s and painkillers were poorly understood. Over the ensuing years she became reliant, then addicted to the medication, eventually adding alcohol to the mix.

When I was young I didn't know anything of her experiences or the reasons for her behaviour. All I knew was the pain of a little girl whose mother was distant and seemed uninvested in her happiness. Suffering through my own tough experiences as an adult, I developed a deep empathy for my mother. I'm sure her upbringing left her tormented by self-doubt just like me. We never talked about it, but we definitely coped with it differently. My mother undoubtedly deserves more credit than my imperfect memories could possibly afford her. She was loved by many of her friends and all of her family.

By the time my parents visited for the intervention order hearing, I hadn't been alone with my mother for many years. While Stuart and Dad stood beside the barbeque nursing a beer and flipping meat, I took the opportunity to settle down on the couch beside Mum. She tried to steer the conversation to her usual criticisms (this time I could only agree with her judgement that I looked dreadful), but I wasn't going to let the opportunity pass us by. I needed to say the words I'd been bottling up inside for most of my life. She sat quietly without interrupting as I explained why I never confided in her; how she never made me feel supported and it always felt like she was pushing me away; that her criticism of me was unfair and I'd been through hell; that I felt abandoned by her too many times. "Mum, why have you never supported me? Why have you never been proud of me?"

Usually she was quick to defend herself, but for a moment there was a rare silence. She'd been well-practiced at filling silence with tension and unspoken threats too, but this was different. I felt none of the usual foreboding. The silence was almost comforting.

She slowly reached out a hand to touch my knee. "I *am* proud of you.

I'm sorry." Then she leaned in to wrap her arms around me, and we sat softly entwined for an eternal moment. I sank into the warm comfort of my mother's arms. It was the most natural of acts, but one I found hard to recall from my childhood. Our mother-daughter bond, hijacked by generations of pain, felt magically intact.

But now my mother was gone.

～

I was desperate to be with my dad. I'd never heard his voice sound so broken. "I woke up to hear her gasping for air and I called an ambulance. When they got here she went into cardiac arrest. They tried to save her, but she passed away."

I told him I would be there as soon as I could, then I quickly phoned Stuart. He and Sophie had arrived at the shops but immediately turned back. I grabbed my computer and tried logging in to book a flight, but I was too shaken to perform even this simple task. Giving up, I rang the hotline, explaining to the voice on the end of the line that my mother had unexpectedly passed away and I needed to get myself and my daughter there without delay. The operator was fantastic, booking us on a flight leaving just two and a half hours later.

Stuart and Sophie came through the door while I was flinging clothes into a case. Sophie was a mess; tears streamed down her face as she threw herself into my arms. I held her, praying this sudden new ordeal would not destroy her. All my children were close to my parents. Regardless of the issues between me and my mother, when it came to her grandchildren, she was always there for them. During the years when I was running my business she was like their second mum, and they called her Mama.

Stuart dropped us at the airport and we rushed through security, boarding the flight with only minutes to spare. Once we'd settled in for the two-hour flight, we didn't speak much. Whenever my thoughts turned to my mother I could feel the choking grief grab at my throat, but I was more concerned how Sophie was handling her grief. She was tense and agitated, and I distracted myself by watching her and trying to read her emotions.

By the time we arrived at my parent's home, Mum's body had already been taken away, but even as I held my dad tight, I was overcome by the smell of her perfume. It triggered the strongest sensation of her presence. I ran to her bedroom hoping it was all a bad dream, hoping she would be sitting there ready to question my hastily selected fashion choices. I would have given anything for that. Throwing myself on her bed, I buried my head in her pillow and breathed her essence deep into my lungs. I broke down, calling out to her, begging her to come back; there was still so much I needed to say. "Please, Mum, please. I need you now more than ever. I'm struggling; struggling to keep Sophie safe; struggling to make decisions; struggling with life. Don't do this now. My family needs you. I need you!"

My dad was forlorn. His wife of fifty years was gone. I couldn't imagine the feeling. I'd never seen him waver in his steadfast commitment to his wife. It must have been difficult for him when Mum's behaviour drove a wedge between family members, but he'd stuck by her. All Sophie and I could do was sit with him, make him a cup of tea, encourage him to eat and help him work through all the decisions he would now be forced to make. It kept us busy which was a relief, but there were plenty of lonely moments in the quiet house for us to all get lost in our reflections and our sorrow.

After returning home from meeting with the church minister one evening, Dad and I sat in the kitchen discussing the arrangements for the service. Suddenly I jumped up in fright. "Where's Sophie?" I asked anxiously. I'd stopped watching her for a few minutes and I realised she was in the shower. "Oh no ..." I ran down the hallway to the ensuite and found her on the floor of the shower, propped up against the wall.

The water running over her body was flowing in a crimson stream to the drain.

"Sophie, no!"

I quickly turned the water off and draped a towel over her as Dad came running through the door. He stood frozen in shock at the sight. Stuart and I had explained to Dad that she would always cut herself in the shower and how terrifying it was for us. Now he was seeing it with his own eyes for the first time.

He helped me get Sophie out of the shower and we pressed towels on her wounds. Because my mother had been a nurse, he found everything we needed in his first aid cupboard. "I'll take it from here love," Dad said, tenderly leading Sophie into the bedroom where he taped up her ghastly wounds and soothed her with his magical words of wisdom. I went back into the bathroom to clean up the bloody mess of self-hatred left in the wake of my daughter's grief. Alone, with my body still shaking from the shock, I talked to Mum. I begged her not to desert me. "I need you. Please help me fix this." In that cold, quiet space I needed to believe someone might be watching over us, and while my bond with my mother had been fragile, it was reassuring enough to get me off the floor and keep me going.

Once Sophie was bandaged up, I decided to give her a sleeping tablet. I was exhausted and it was the only way either of us were going to get any sleep. When I was sure she wasn't going to move from her bed, I sat with Dad. He was devastated by what he'd just witnessed. My dad is the most stoic man I know. I'd rarely seen him shed a tear, but here he was facing the loss of his wife and also witnessing the struggle and torment of his granddaughter. He choked up with tears and vowed he would do whatever it took, whatever Sophie, Stuart and I needed, to help get her through this. After the long months of navigating our strange new life alone, it felt good to have support from someone close to us who understood what we were going through.

Two days later we laid Mum to rest. The church was packed and there were even people standing outside. It was wonderful to see the care and support shown for Dad, and I know Mum would have been so happy. I hoped she was there. I believe she was.

The following day we flew home. It was difficult to leave Dad but I knew our bond was stronger than ever. Our relationship had been strained many times throughout my life, but I was beginning to understand the impossible choices Mum had forced upon him. Her complex personality and judgmental nature required subtle navigation, and only a patient and steady man like my father could have sustained such a relationship. He was devoted to her, and somehow he remained devoted to us kids even when Mum gave him ultimatums. While his presence in my life sometimes faded, I never felt that he deserted me. Now, even overcome by his grief, his desire to be there for us was obvious. I might have lost my mother, but in a strange twist, her death gave me back my father.

Chapter 12
Groundhog Day

An uneasy routine settled over our days. After the series of shocks we'd encountered during the past four months, it may have looked like we finally had space to breathe, but nothing could be further from the truth. There was too much time to dwell, and Sophie struggled anew with her efforts to return to school and re-engage with life. She was still in regular therapy, but we were out of the loop and had no idea if she was making progress. Even though I'd battled through my own tough years, I felt useless. I wanted to pull her through as quickly as possible. I wanted to help her avoid more pain. I wanted it all to be behind her, but there is no shortcut through trauma. Once those emotions locked deep down inside find their way to the surface, they roll through like storms, wild and tumultuous.

Sophie would have a series of emotionally sunny days when she would go to school, play with Buddy, engage in conversations with us, and let a little smile or laugh brighten her gorgeous face. The glimmer of happiness gave me hope; *Maybe the worst was behind her.* But I eventually realised this period was the calm before the storm. Even while soaking up these fragments of joy, I learnt to scan for warning signs that she was slipping. Stuart and I became familiar with the pattern and could predict a storm's arrival.

First her mood would darken. Self-doubt and confusion seemed to build like clouds on the horizon, obstructing her radiance and sucking her back into whatever thoughts troubled her mind. She would become irritable, and every little thing we did annoyed her. What brought her joy just days earlier, seemed suddenly intolerable. I knew we were at this point when even Buddy's adoring puppy face couldn't elicit a pat. Stuart and I would feel the pressure of the mounting emotional storm and it made us extremely apprehensive.

Getting her up and off to school became more and more difficult. Before preparing for work, I would go into her room and sit with her to see how she was feeling, trying to judge if it would be safe to leave her. When it wasn't, Stuart and I would take turns to stay home, knowing she was too fragile to be left alone with only the hollow echoes of an empty house for company. We didn't always get it right. I vividly recall days when I arrived at work, only to receive the dreaded 9am automated text message from the school advising me Sophie had not turned up. A call to her phone would inevitably go unanswered. Trying to remain composed, I'd quietly advise my loyal assistant I needed to leave urgently. By the time I reached my car, my heart was in my throat and the thin veneer of calm was gone. Racing home while vainly calling her number, I tormented myself with visions of what I might be about to walk into, always imagining the worst as I pulled into the driveway.

I'm grateful those desperate sprints home were never met with one of the horrific scenes conjured by my overactive mind, but nothing could dampen the anxiety I would feel the next time, and the next time, and the next. During these turbulent periods I would once again sleep on the floor outside her door, too afraid I might not be there when she needed me. I regularly searched her room for anything she could use to self-harm. Desperate to find some relief from her overwhelming mental anguish, this was when she would be at greatest risk of cutting herself.

Hearing her bathroom door slam one morning, I rushed up the stairs and heard heartbreaking sobs through the door. I walked in, fearful I might be too late to avert another shocking episode. Instead I found her sitting on the closed toilet, hands clenched tightly on her lap as she rocked back and forth. She looked up at me, her face flushed red and smeared wet with tears. Through her sobs I could hear moaning; "Why did this happen to me? Someone must have known. They would have heard. Why didn't anyone come and save me? Why didn't *you* save me? I want the pain to go away." I knelt quickly by her side, then saw she was scratching at her skin, leaving deep red welts beside the scars already marking her porcelain white thighs. I grabbed her hands and forced her to take my arms. "Hurt me," I begged, and she did, screaming while she squeezed so hard I thought my bones might break. But I would bear any pain for her, and I pleaded in silent desperation to any higher force that might be listening for my daughter to be saved from this cruel punishment. As I felt her tension subside, I pulled her into my arms and we slid slowly onto the floor, hugging until our breathing slowed and stillness settled over our weary bodies.

While Sophie's outbursts frightened me, I preferred them to the silence of her complete withdrawal, which is generally what came next. Worn out, she would lie unmoving on her bed for hours – sometimes days – crying quietly. It was as if the swollen rain clouds had finally broken, spilling their sadness and despair in a steady stream of tears. The retreat into her unresolved pain was all-consuming. She would not leave her room. She would not speak to us. My father had religiously called Sophie every morning after Mum's funeral, sharing motivational quotes and encouraging her to stay positive. He was keen to do anything to keep her engaged in life, and the routine seemed healing for them both. But she wouldn't answer his calls when she was drowning in the emotional storm. The fight would go out of her eyes, all hope lost, and I could feel her sliding precariously close to the edge of that cliff. This is when I truly knew fear. This is when we really needed help.

Over the next few months, Dr Rama admitted Sophie for extended stays at the clinic four times. It felt like a defeat every time, but knowing she was safe there was also a relief. Stuart and I could recover our lost sleep, and for a few days I appreciated the opportunity to get through a meeting without being on edge. But for us it was only the eye of the storm, a quiet moment to take stock. My anxiety remained high as I wondered constantly how she was feeling and yearned to be near her. Days were a blur of long work hours, quick visits to Sophie at lunchtime, and longer visits with Stuart after work. By the time we got home, had dinner and caught up on our chores, we'd both collapse into bed exhausted. Lying there, waiting for sleep to bring its blessed relief, the same question would circle through my mind; *When will this end?* I couldn't see a finish line and I became more discouraged each time she was admitted. I found it harder to maintain my stubborn faith that things would eventually be okay.

When Sophie was at her lowest, sometimes I would lie in bed with her while she sobbed. I wanted so desperately to understand what was happening to her, to gain some insight into the thoughts and feelings driving her to the edge of the cliff, but I never asked. I wanted it to be her decision to involve me, because every time I tried to be the fixer, I ended up pushing too hard and dreading I might have gone too far. One night she did open up. "I hate myself. Sometimes I want to end it all." While this was devastating enough, she went on to reveal more about the conflict consuming her innocent little soul. She still loved her father and desperately wanted his unconditional love, despite all he did to her.

There was a tug-of-war going on inside her. How could anyone make sense of that clash of emotions at any age, let alone at the vulnerable age of seventeen? I certainly couldn't. My experience of leaving him hadn't been textbook. I'd buried my pain deep inside and swept my conflicting emotions under the carpet. I knew how confusing it was to seesaw between love and disgust, anger and despair. Now I was watching a similar battle of emotions play out within my precious child. While I had avoided diving into my trauma, she was drowning in hers. I didn't know how to help her.

As the days went on, I began to spiral. The rage I felt towards her father spread like a virus, infecting my cells with anger and loathing, but all it did was make me hate myself. I was suffocating in a thick smog of blame and regret. My daughter was suffering and I didn't do anything – still couldn't do anything – to ease her pain. I felt useless, totally helpless and utterly hopeless. I understood for the first time the emptiness in Sophie's eyes. Dark thoughts now settled heavily in my own mind. I lay awake outside her door contemplating what I should do. All her medications were locked away. I could easily give both of us a handful of tablets to end all the pain and suffering. Together we could escape this prison. There seemed to be no other way out.

I wasn't prepared for the depression. For the last few months I'd been gripped by anxiety, which prodded me to keep searching for answers and keep moving forward. Anxiety arises from obsessive worrying about the future, but depression arises from dwelling on the past. Sophie was captured by her irresolvable past, and now I was too. I couldn't see a way forward. My innate optimism had run out, and my natural determination and belief that we could get through this had completely evaporated.

Then I thought of Stuart, my true love. I couldn't do it to him. He was a reason to live, not only for me, but for Sophie too. I honestly believe there's hope for humanity as long as there are men like him in the world. I got up from the hard floor and went downstairs, where I sat on the couch waiting for Stuart to wake. When he came out of the bedroom, he saw me sitting there with eyes puffy from crying all night. He sat beside me and I shared the thoughts that were visiting me in the dark hours. "I can't go on and I feel there's only one option left."

He held me tight and said, "I've got a better option."

He phoned work to tell them he wouldn't be in. At 8:30am he phoned our doctor's office. They knew what we were going through with Sophie and they told him to bring me straight in. While Sophie stayed in the waiting room, Stuart and I sat with our amazing doctor who listened attentively and then spoke; "You already know this, Rose, but I'll say it anyway. Suicide doesn't end the chances of life getting worse, it destroys the possibility of it ever getting better." I was in crisis and I knew my depression wouldn't disappear without an intervention. I had witnessed Sophie's struggle with her surging emotions and was ready to do whatever my doctor suggested. If I ignored these grim feelings, things would get worse, not only for me, but also for my loved ones.

My doctor proposed medication and I was initially reluctant, recalling how Sophie had appeared so dull and lifeless when it was first prescribed for her. I didn't want to feel that way, but there was more to it. Despite everything I was learning about mental health on the journey with Sophie, I felt the sharp sting of judgement arise in my mind. Taking medication seemed like surrendering to something I should have been able to conquer on my own. I immediately knew this thought was wrong, an echo of the ill-informed prejudices that infect our society. When I was growing up, any sign of emotional struggle was met with insensitive comments such as 'harden up!'. It's difficult to shake these ingrained attitudes even when you know better, but I was spiralling down and it was not something I could beat without support. I was lucky my husband responded immediately to my cry for help and took me to a doctor who listened and cared. I wish I had done this earlier for Sophie, and maybe we could have averted the worst of her anguish.

Medication took the power out of the insidious thoughts threatening to drag me under. As they subsided, I regained control over my mind. I was able to make some important lifestyle changes, the first of which was cutting back on alcohol. It was a prop I put in my hand every night, relying on it to bring some lightness to those heavy days. It was a con and I knew it. I also changed my eating habits. I'd been grabbing fast calories in my rush from home to work, to the clinic and back, and I'd put on weight. It added to my depressive state, so I went back to basics, cooking at home and paying more attention to my portion sizes. Factoring a little bit of time into my day to make a healthy meal felt good. I returned to the gym, training five days per week. Stuart had maintained his gym habit the whole time, but mine fell away quickly during Sophie's first stay in the clinic.

I also saw a counsellor. I knew my depression had its roots in painful events that occurred much earlier in my life, but I wasn't ready to prioritise my own trauma. Instead I focused on getting through the immediate challenges with my counsellor. I picked up some helpful tools from the sessions such as journalling and writing down three things I was grateful for each day. I began to appreciate the smallest moments in my day, such as a break in the rain just when I needed to dash from my car to a building; the feel of Buddy's soft fur as he rubbed against my leg; the taste of a ripe new-season peach. I realised my life was full of wonderful things.

After two months, I'd lost 9kg and increased my fitness. On most days my head felt clear and my sleep improved dramatically. I was less fixated on our problems and more aware of the positive things happening around me. The change in my mindset and the improvement in my physical condition felt great. I still had anxious days and sometimes felt overwhelmed, but I was more able to deal with it. My doctor worked with me to cut back the medication, and I eventually stopped completely.

I was determined to continue these healthy habits, even more so when I noticed my actions were having a positive influence on Sophie. She was making better food choices and sometimes joined me at the gym. She also began journalling. If I couldn't fix things for her, maybe fixing my life would encourage her to believe she could find her own way back from the edge.

Chapter 13
Breakthrough

Real breakthroughs are messy. Sophie's first significant step forward came when I was convinced she was sliding backwards. We were caught in another emotional storm cycle and Sophie spent the weekend in bed. On Monday morning it was obvious I couldn't leave her alone. She'd stopped eating, talking or even acknowledging me. Without hesitation I phoned Dr Rama who decided we should get her to hospital immediately. She would check to see if there was a place at the clinic and call me back. I went up to Sophie's room to tell her, but she didn't react. When Dr Rama rang back she told me the clinic was full and I would need to call an ambulance so Sophie could be taken to the nearest public hospital. "But Rose, while I was on the phone to the clinic they advised me Sophie's father has been calling trying to get information. There is an alert on their system because of the intervention order, but has it been served on him?"

"I'm not certain, but I would have thought so. I'll see what I can find out." As I hung up I felt the first stirrings of frustration. I was already annoyed about missing work and disturbed by Sophie's stonewalling. Now my buried anger for her father was rising fast.

I immediately called the ambulance and was advised it could take an hour for one to arrive. I was offered the opportunity to speak with a mental health nurse while we waited. When I explained our situation to the nurse, she asked if she could speak with Sophie. I returned to the bedroom and held the phone to Sophie's ear, but she remained silent. Realising she may be more inclined to talk if I wasn't in the room, I rested the phone beside her ear and walked out.

I sat where I had sat countless times before, at the top of the stairs waiting. Moments later I could hear Sophie's voice as she responded to the nurse. After a few muffled sentences her voice got louder.

"I hate my mother! I hate my father! My father abused me for as long as I can remember."

I was unprepared for the shock of discovering more horrific details this way. *How young was she? How long did this go on?*

Terror, hatred and repulsion swept through my body and I started to shake with pure rage. *You fucking son of a bitch. You piece of shit! How dare you do this to my daughter, how fucking dare you?* My mind was on fire; a white-hot cauldron of vengeful thoughts flickering without form. I lost track of time, no longer able to hear Sophie's voice. Rage consumed me until the sound of knocking on the front door stirred me from my fiery hell.

The paramedics took Sophie to the nearby hospital. I told them I would follow shortly but had to do something on my way. Turning left as they turned right, I drove straight to the local police station. The officer at the desk became the target for my anger. I demanded they put a stop to Sophie's father before I got on a plane and went there to finish him off once and for all. In hindsight, I was lucky the officer was an understanding young man who seemed to quickly sense the pain of a parent caught in a difficult situation. I hate to think what I'd have done if he hadn't reassured me they would handle it.

When I arrived at the hospital I was told to take a seat. I looked around at the cold, sterile waiting room, its hard blue seats occupied by a wide array of humanity. But it was not their differences that stood out to me, it was the similarity of their postures; elbows resting on thighs, heads lowered to avoid eye contact. It's the resigned stance of those whose lives have been put on hold, knowing the wait will be long and they can do nothing to influence it. It was all too familiar to me, and I knew their outward stillness was a facade, hiding minds full of anxiety and uncertainty. I'd been there too many times and today I couldn't join them in the charade. Instead I paced up and down the long corridor, my anger yet to abate and my mind running at high speed on a repeating track: *Enough. It has to end. We can't keep doing this.* I needed a calming voice and went outside to call Stuart. When he didn't answer, I called my other rock, my dad.

The moment I heard his voice I burst into tears. I felt a sudden pang of nostalgic longing for my childhood when he could wrap me in his arms and make everything better, just the way he did when I fell and scraped my knees. The feeling was overpowering, a pull to the past when my pain was easily mended. But I was a big girl now, a thousand miles away from my dad's secure arms, facing a never-ending nightmare. I knew it was my job to get my child through this, but I didn't know how.

It's funny how some of the most useful advice comes when you least expect it. Despite all the experts treating Sophie (but not communicating much with us), it was my dad who helped me understand Sophie's outburst might be a good sign. He'd recently lunched with an acquaintance who was previously in the Child Protection Unit of the Police Department. He explained to Dad how child sexual abuse victims often blame the non-offending parent for not protecting them, and if she was able to verbalise it, that meant she was starting to get it out and deal with it. I really hoped he was right. So far the suggestion of blame had hung heavily in her silence, but she was definitely beginning to express it now. I didn't know how to prepare myself for what might come next, but no matter how tough her accusations, or how much she declared her hatred for me, I knew I couldn't let her push me away. She needed me to be strong and prove I would never leave her side. To abandon her in the face of her fury would only reinforce her fears. I knew I could endure it because my role model was right there on the phone. All my life my father never wavered in his love and loyalty to us children, no matter what my brothers and I threw at him, and no matter what my mum demanded of him. He always turned the other cheek and continued to love us unconditionally. Dad gave me the courage I desperately needed to get myself and my daughter through this.

When I was called in to speak with the doctor, he told me Sophie was fine. She said she wouldn't harm herself, and he was happy for her to leave. I looked him straight in the eye as mine welled with tears, and pleaded with him, "Please, you don't understand, she has attempted suicide before. I know her – she is so withdrawn. She is close to doing it again. Have you seen her legs and her stomach? Barely a week goes by where she doesn't hack herself to pieces."

"No I haven't," he admitted.

Distraught, I continued, "Please, I'm begging you to admit her. I can no longer keep her safe. My husband and I have tried everything and I've got nothing left. You have to understand, she has no will, nothing left to live for. She will tell you whatever she has to, so you'll let her go and she can end her life."

He paused, clearly contemplating my words. "Okay, I'll order a psych review." *Thank God.* I nearly collapsed with relief. That would keep her safe until we could get her back under Dr Rama's care. I returned to the waiting room, now exhausted from my spent emotions. I sat in one of the hard blue seats and assumed the same resigned position as my anonymous companions.

The minutes dragged into hours as I waited for yet another assessment of my daughter to be completed. Waiting is torture for me. Too much time to think and not enough action. I'm only hopeful when I can sense progress is being made, but I struggled to find any sign of headway in this situation. Although I'd made positive steps forward in my mental state, these situations immediately plunged me back into anxiety. I was agitated, my thinking scattered, my heart rate elevated and my nerves on edge.

When I was eventually called back to Sophie's room, I found her sitting on the bed with the psychiatrist standing beside her. "Rose, Sophie has something to tell you."

Not more revelations, I thought. *What else could there be?*

My sweet daughter looked up, her swollen, red eyes struggling to focus on me. Then she yelled, her voice full of rage, "I hate you for what you've done! You let him do this to me. You wanted him to do it. You were a part of his sick plan."

I felt dizzy, as if her words had sucked the air from the room. It was the sharpest cut, a knife driving straight into my heart and releasing all the guilt and regret I'd buried deep inside.

My response was automatic, a pitiful plea for understanding; "I didn't know. If I'd known I would have taken you away and protected you." Even as the words came, I sensed their futility. She didn't want my explanation, she just needed to express her sense of abandonment.

She screamed back at me, "The signs were there! They were all there and you did nothing."

I felt the relentless waves of remorse pound me. She was right. The signs were there and I was too ignorant to notice. How could I have been so foolish? How could I have been so pathetic and incompetent as a mother? Above all else, the one thing I wanted for my children was a warm, loving and ever-present mother. How could I have created the very same hurt my own mother had left as a scar inside me – the hollow pain of abandonment?

I could find no words to offer her, but before I succumbed fully to my anguish, Sophie's face crumbled as the rage left her body. She burst into tears and reached her arms up to me, the same way she did when she was a baby. "I'm so sorry, Mum, I'm so sorry. Please forgive me. I know you didn't know. I have so much hatred inside, and I'm directing it all at you when it should be at him."

⁓

I've spent many sleepless hours wondering why I missed the signs that something was wrong inside my family. Maybe it was because too many things were wrong. I was so focused on the problems in my marriage, it blinded me to wider dangers. I now believe his emotional and psychological mistreatment of me was partly designed to distract me from his appalling behaviour outside the home and from his shocking secret inside it. I was naive, too easily rendered powerless by the sly manipulation, cruel gaslighting and subtle ridicule. Once I saw it clearly, it only made me feel more guilty for being so unaware. Eventually I would peel those layers back and find a strong, clear-minded and confident woman beneath, but it would take time.

⁓

Something broke that day, but it wasn't our relationship or Sophie's will to live. Somehow her outburst unlocked a door she needed to pass through. I thought it was the lowest point, but it was actually a turning point. This was to be Sophie's last stay in hospital.

When we lifted our heads after shedding tears in a tight embrace, the psychiatrist explained to Sophie that reporting the crime was the only way she would get closure. It would help her regain control and begin to heal. The psychiatrist was obliged to submit a report to the police, and within a week I received a call from the team who deal with child abuse claims. Sophie decided she was ready to make a formal report so we arranged a time to meet them.

Stuart and I were extremely supportive of Sophie's quest for justice, but we were also cautious. We were still in protective mode and concerned this step could put her under a lot of pressure. It would require a significant degree of courage and fortitude, attributes I knew Sophie possessed, but hadn't shown since she'd attempted to take her life. Could she find her strength again? As I drove her to meet with the police, I reminded her if she found any of it too difficult she could always pull out. "We're beside you no matter what," I told her, hoping she didn't hear the fear and doubt in my voice. I worried the legal system might be a tough place for a girl who was teetering on the edge. But there was something different about her that day. She was sitting up straight and looked like a girl on a mission. The air of defeat that had clung to her for months was gone, and in its place was a fresh determination.

"I know, Mum, but it's okay. I want to do it," she replied.

Two young female detectives greeted us. I'm guessing they had chosen this line of work by the attentive way they ushered us through the corridors and took the time to make sure we were comfortable and relaxed. They were confident young women, but also displayed a tenderness that put my mind at ease. *Maybe this is a good idea,* I thought, but then they explained the process. One would interview Sophie and the other would interview me. *Wait, what? They want to interview me?* I wasn't prepared for that. To ensure Sophie's case was properly prepared, one of the detectives explained, they needed to gather as much information as possible. Nervous, but determined to help in any way I could, I followed her into a tiny windowless room while the other detective led Sophie to a room further down the corridor. At first the detective asked me a few simple questions such as where I lived and what sort of work I did, then she probed into details of my previous marriage and the children's upbringing. My mind raced, unsure what was expected of me. Did they want the short version or the long one?

Finally she asked about Sophie's father and how he treated me. I told her he had never been abusive to me, by which I meant he hadn't ever hit me. But as she dug deeper and I opened up about the way our marriage fell apart, she explained there are many forms of domestic violence, and just because he hadn't laid a hand on me, it didn't mean he wasn't abusive. My interview took about an hour, and after I finished giving my statement I was led back to the waiting room.

Sitting alone waiting for Sophie, I reflected on the detective's comments. Why had it taken me so long to realise I was a victim of domestic violence? I knew he treated me badly over the years, but I'd never let myself call it abuse. Having someone sit in front of me and explain the range of behaviours police consider when assessing domestic and family violence, I recognised many of these forms of abuse from my marriage. The belittling statements, the sexual pressure, the way he shifted blame to me for any problems in the family, the threats when I tried to end our marriage, the way he put me down and played mind games that completely undermined of my sense of self – these were the ways he exerted power and control over me. And behind the curtain of all the mistreatment lay the worst crime of all; the sexual abuse of an innocent little girl, his own daughter.

Was it ignorance that blinded me to the reality of my situation? Naivety or weakness? Or did I fall for the foolish belief that 'it couldn't happen to me'? Early in our marriage I was happy enough, but these behaviours emerged slowly. I was the proverbial frog in boiling water, not realising the temperature was rising, or noticing when my nerves tingled with pain and my muscles twitched in agony. By then he had convinced me I couldn't survive without him, and I convinced myself it was best for the children if I stayed. And I slowly began to drown.

~

Sophie's interview took six hours. When the detective came to find me in the waiting room she said, "Sophie's nearly finished. We are printing out her statement and once she signs it you'll be able to leave. She did an amazing job."

"I know you can't say too much but please tell me, is it serious?" As soon as the question passed my lips, I was concerned she might think I didn't believe Sophie, but that wasn't it at all. After months of being kept in the dark, I think I needed someone who knew all the details to validate what we were going through. I often doubted myself and whether I was making the right decisions, but I never doubted Sophie. Maybe a small part of me hoped someone would tell me it was all a nightmare and shake me back to reality, but I knew that was just a pipedream.

"Rose, it is very serious. Sophie has been extremely courageous, recalling events in such detail. Her story has stayed the same throughout, and we believe she is telling the truth. In fact, we asked if she would do a pretext phone call, and she agreed."

"What's a pretext phone call?" I asked warily.

"It is where we connect her phone to a recording device and she calls the perpetrator to confront him. We hope he will say something incriminating, or even admit to the crime. It can be quite helpful in cases like this."

Her answer didn't put my mind at ease. In fact, I was now very nervous. "It doesn't sound like a great idea. What if it tips her over the edge? I am so supportive of Sophie's plight for justice, but not if it puts her life at more risk. What if I did it instead?"

"We could do that Rose, but the whole idea is for the call to come from the victim. He knows only he and Sophie were there when the crimes took place, which means the chances he will incriminate himself are better if she confronts him."

"Okay. Can we at least have some time to discuss it with Sophie?"

"Of course, take your time and do what is best for Sophie. Many victims find it too confronting; we understand that."

Before long, Sophie appeared from the interview room. Her eyes were puffy, reminding me of a fighter who'd just done ten rounds in the boxing ring. She was completely drained, and I wrapped an arm around her as I led her gently to the car.

Over the next week we saw a shift in Sophie. She held her head a little higher and her voice was clearer and stronger. The quest for justice against the man who so brutally violated her from such a young age gave her purpose. Her strong will was returning and she had some fight back. Now she was directing her anger, blame and disgust towards the person who was responsible for her pain and trauma, rather than towards herself. While there were still times when her spirit dived, we sensed she had reached an important turning point.

I took Sophie back to the station for the pretext phone call the following week. She was very anxious because she hadn't spoken to her father in many months, but she was determined to do it. "Mum, I have to do this. I have to do whatever I can to stand up to him."

A detective took her into a recording room to set everything up, then came out to sit with me. "She must be completely alone when she makes the call." She explained how most victims, including many adults much older than Sophie, cannot bring themselves to do it. She thought Sophie was incredibly strong.

That's my girl, I thought with pride. She was facing one of the most challenging things any human being could do, entering a wolf's lair armed only with a belief in the power of good over evil. I never would have believed it possible just weeks earlier.

After a fairly short time, Sophie opened the door and walked down the corridor towards us looking dejected. Despite making a couple of calls, he did not answer. When Stuart bought Sophie the new phone a few months earlier, she'd set her number to appear as an unknown caller. She didn't want her father to know her new number, but now he wasn't picking up the call. She felt deflated, however the detectives decided to send her home with the recording device and instructions on how to use it. She could try again in her own time, but they reminded her she must be alone when making the call.

We drove home in silence. Sophie was anxious. I could read her like a book now; it was more than her body language or her tone of voice. I could feel her energy whenever she was near me. Whatever she felt, I would feel it too. I cautiously broke the silence. "Honey, if it's is too hard you know you don't have to do it."

"You don't understand, Mum, I have to do this."

The thing is, I did understand. After hiding her pain from the world, she had reached a point in her journey where she was no longer willing to stay silent. It was the point I also reached with my mother before she passed away, a yearning for my pain to be acknowledged. I wasn't searching for a way to punish my mother. I still loved her. For me, the small but sincere 'sorry' was enough to help me begin dealing with the shame and rejection I'd been carrying since I was a child.

I clearly remember Sophie standing in front of me pleading, "Mum, why can't he admit what he has done to me and say sorry? Why can't he speak the truth? If he could just do that, I would have peace and I wouldn't have to go down this path. It's causing so much pain for everyone. It's killing me."

I knew exactly how she felt. It's hell when the person who has hurt you so badly is someone you still love. Your heart feels like it's being torn apart. You want to hear them admit you were wronged. You want them to tell you it was never your fault. Until they take responsibility and express their guilt, you carry those things on yourself, believing you somehow deserved whatever crimes were committed against you. It's incredibly difficult to move forward until you are freed from that burden. But what can you do if they refuse? How can you move on when you are tethered by love to someone who is unwilling to show you a healthy love in return?

On the following Sunday, after rising early and cleaning the house, I went out for groceries while Stuart stayed home with Sophie. When I walked back through the door carrying the heavy bags, I wondered why Stuart didn't meet me to help as he usually did. Walking further into the house, I could sense something was wrong. I found them in the lounge room sitting on the couch, Stuart with his arm around Sophie who was sobbing quietly. Stuart's warm blue eyes met mine, telling me in his comforting way – *don't worry, everything is okay.* "Sophie just phoned him," he said.

She jumped up and launched herself into my arms. I couldn't imagine how much courage it had taken for her to make that call. With every sob her body shuddered and I held her close, wishing I could absorb her pain.

Chapter 14
Family Matters

We rang the police to explain what happened and they told us to come in immediately. Sophie wasn't confident the recording was worthwhile, and she said very little as we drove to the police station. The superintendent took the recording away to check it and soon returned with a smile on his face. "Bingo, we have him. The prosecutor listened to it and believes it strongly supports her statement."

He crouched in front of Sophie and looked directly into her eyes. "Sophie, you are one strong and amazing young woman. It's extremely confronting to face a perpetrator, but you did it." The tension in her face melted away. I was so relieved the gamble had paid off, but as we returned home I wondered what lay ahead. *Will justice be served? What price will Sophie have to pay? Will it be worth it in the end?*

⌒〜

It took another two years before Sophie's case was heard in court.

The case was handed over to the Child Protection Unit in the State where we lived when Sophie was little. We had no idea how the legal system worked and there was little communication from the investigating detectives or the prosecutor assigned to the case. Sophie, Stuart and I were all asked a number of times to provide statements, but between those rare approaches from the legal team we were left in the dark. We waited in nervous anticipation for updates that never came, and my attempts to find out more were met with little response. Lack of clarity is perfect fodder for anxiety and I was constantly on edge, uneasy about how this prolonged uncertainty would affect my daughter.

While I worried about Sophie, she was concerned about us. I saw so much of myself in her during that time. We were both people pleasers, putting the feelings and needs of others ahead of our own. Perhaps I'd raised her to be the perfect victim. She had seen me keep secrets just to keep the peace, but secrets are crazy-making stuff. I wished I could go back in time and teach her how to put herself first. I especially wished I had taught her not to do anything that made her feel uncomfortable just to please someone else. Even as I thought all this, I knew I was slipping right back into the pattern myself. I was preoccupied with saving her and I neglected myself. Guilt, regret and anxiety returned to haunt me. We needed a way to lift our sights beyond the court case and rebuild our lives. That's when we made a decision I look back on as one of the best we've ever made: we started family counselling.

Sophie, Stuart and I met with two counsellors every fortnight. In my experience, there is some luck involved in finding the right people at the right time. Sophie was with her original psychologist for about six months, but felt she wasn't making much progress. Our doctor referred her to a new one who turned out to be magic, and she also arranged our family sessions. To sit together and share our fears in a safe space with such caring guidance was truly amazing. We'd all been holding back our raw emotions, but these sessions helped us to understand each other. We could also be honest about the support we needed from each other.

Sophie made it clear she just needed us to be there without judgement. I could do that. But the biggest lightbulb moment was when she asked me to stop trying to fix her and save her. It didn't help; in fact, it often made things worse. I knew this had been my biggest stumbling block all along, but I didn't understand how damaging it was until she raised it. My well-intentioned efforts to dive in and fix everything completely disempowered her. It was impossible for her to learn how to navigate her own challenges. She couldn't develop the very thing she needed to get through her life; resilience. I was also damaging myself. Constantly striving to fix things meant I never gave myself the time or space to sit with a problem and truly understand it. I was pushing away the very opportunities all of us were being offered to learn and grow. Ironically, my desire to fix everything was keeping us stuck.

I could see it, but gee, it was difficult to change it. I noticed how much I struggled to simply sit and listen to Sophie. My mind would jump ahead and I was never in the moment. I also noticed this seemed to be the source of my anxiety. Once Sophie explained why she needed me to let go, I realised she was giving me a gift. It was something I had to do for my own mental health as well as hers.

The family sessions gave me an opportunity to say things I had been too frightened to voice before. I'd been masking my emotions around Sophie, worried my words or actions could push her over the edge. Once I felt that it was safe to reveal my true feelings, there was something I wanted Sophie to understand. No longer could I hide my constant dread that she would hurt herself or step off the cliff again. I'd been holding it in for so long, but with the two counsellors to guide us, I was able to finally express my fear.

My eyes welled with tears and my bottom lip began to quiver as I looked at my sweet girl. "Sophie, I need you to understand how I feel. I live in constant fear. Every time I arrive in our driveway, or reach out to open your bedroom door, my heart begins to race. I don't know what

I'll find. I'm afraid you will finally succeed in taking your life. I am so full of guilt and regret; guilt that I never saved you from him, and regret that I can't go back and change it. I can't go back, but *I* can change. You will never know how much I love you until the day you have a child of your own. I love you so much that my heart aches when yours does, I feel everything you feel and I would lay down my life to take your pain away. I can't live without you. My life is nothing without you in it. I am begging you, please promise me you will never take my baby away from me. Promise me when it gets too tough you will talk to me or Dad. Look me in the eye and promise me!"

The tears were streaming down Sophie's face and she stared directly into my eyes, her face full of resolve. I could see she was determined to support me the way I was supporting her. "I promise, Mum. I promise."

Sophie, Stuart and I cried and held each other close. It was another breakthrough, and Sophie's commitment would stand the test of time. She came to us many times to share her anxiety, to talk through her fears and to ask for help. And I tried very hard to be there without fixing it all.

⁓

There was a surreal edge to our lives. Waiting for the court case was like living under a cloud. If we'd known the process would take two years, we could have planned our lives around it, but we hesitated from fully embracing life. What we were really waiting for was closure. Even so, we found a rhythm to our lives. Sophie returned to school and our family counselling sessions helped me resist the urge to drag her out of bed and shepherd her like a mother goose. She had to work it out for herself. Once Stuart and I let go of our worries about her results at school and were simply grateful she was alive and healing, I think she felt the pressure come off. That's when she rose to the challenge and her grades began to improve. She loved science, especially biology, and I saw a spark of the little girl who always said she wanted to be a doctor or a nurse. Her school went to great lengths to support Sophie and we were grateful for their understanding. I have no doubt that Sophie's struggles were beyond the job description of most school counsellors. They probably felt out of their depth many times, just as we did. In the end it was up to Sophie to steer her own course, and it's a credit to her strength and determination that she passed year twelve. It was another lesson for me to stop trying to fix things.

The open and understanding communication within our family was a springboard back into life. Stuart and I felt more confident Sophie would be alright when we left her alone or went out for an evening. Home life became lighter and more fun, yet I remained hyper-alert for any signs of fragility. I'd been through a year of heart-stopping setbacks, and anxiety was now my constant companion. It was so familiar I didn't even notice.

I remember stirring lightly from my sleep one night. Sophie had gone out with friends and I didn't hear her come home. My tired eyes tried to make out the time – it was 1:30am. I bolted out of bed and up the stairs, flinging open her bedroom door and flicking on the light. Sophie was tucked up in her big bed alongside one of the other girls and they were both sleeping soundly, or at least they were until I barged in. Her sleepy frown wasn't enough to stop my impassioned plea: "I don't care what time it is, you must wake me up when you come home so I know you are safe. I was scared!"

Our family sessions helped us through these touchy moments. Instead of arguing about things that irritated us, we recognised it was our vulner-abilities speaking, and we approached each other with greater empathy. If our lives had been 'normal', we most likely would never have under-taken those family therapy sessions, which would have been a real shame. I credit them for nurturing the steadfast bond that grew between Sophie and I as she became an adult, and I know they helped Stuart cope with the complex emotions faced by his precious girls.

⁓

I returned to my regular gym sessions and this time Sophie showed much more interest. I think she noticed I was not only physically fitter and healthier, but also much happier. Once she finished her schooling she became a lot more serious about training regularly and eating well. With more time on her hands, she could indulge her interest in holistic health, and she decided she wanted to come off the medication she'd been taking morning and night for the best part of a year. It made her feel numb and detached during the day, and knocked her out at night, inducing a form of sleep that left her feeling flat each morning rather than refreshed. She wanted to get healthy in body and mind, and we could see she was getting stronger.

Sophie raised it a number of times with Dr Rama who, as her psychiatrist, was the one responsible for prescribing her medication, but Dr Rama kept telling her she wasn't ready. She had been wonderful with Sophie in times of crisis, working attentively to adjust her medication and put in place the right supports to guide her safely through the severe risks she faced in the first few months. Maybe she thought the unfinished business of the court case was another big risk, but the work Sophie was doing with the psychologist to face her trauma and summon the courage to report the crimes really changed her. She was inspired to take control of her recovery and she worked hard on her health and fitness over the coming months. When even that didn't persuade Dr Rama to help her come off the medication, we took her back to our lovely local doctor for advice. He listened intently to everything Sophie said and agreed to manage the process of slowly taking her off her medication – on the condition she saw him weekly. Over the coming months, she continued her individual sessions with her psychologist and we came together for our fortnightly family counselling sessions. Our lives revolved around appointments, but it was a jigsaw that fitted together perfectly, and soon Sophie was off all medication and doing incredibly well. She'd done it in a healthy way and felt empowered by reaching her goal. Her eyes were sparkling again and a healthy colour returned to her face. I could feel our lives getting back on track.

Then we opened a gym!

~

Heaven knows what we were thinking. We were enjoying the return of some normality to our lives, including the new-found freedom of not having to worry who was watching Sophie, but there's no doubt Stuart and I were still primarily focused on how to keep her moving forward. For all our sakes, we didn't want her to lose any of the gains she'd made. Nurturing her interest in health and fitness made sense, but rather than encouraging her to seek employment in the field as most parents might do, we built a gym from scratch. I'm sure there were traces of my fixer mentality in the decision, but when a gym closed down nearby, my marketing nose smelt an opportunity. We found a perfect space and fitted it out, launched a big marketing campaign and employed two trainers to run the sessions. And we did all of that while Stuart and I continued to hold down our full-time jobs in busy senior roles. When not at our day jobs, we spent every other waking moment at the gym building the business. Memberships increased so fast that Stuart left his job to run more sessions, and he and Sophie became full-time trainers. They were both very popular, probably because of the huge amount of compassion they showed for other people's personal struggles.

We decided to particularly focus on people who were facing mental health challenges. We knew from our own experience that when you are ready to take control back over your life, exercising can set off a ripple effect, inspiring other healthy habits and triggering positive shifts in mood. We offered fitness classes and functional training, but also nutrition planning and mindset coaching. The demand was there, and we built a reputation for offering a welcoming and supportive environment. I've always loved helping people, and was reminded of the promise I'd made in my letter to Jeff Kennett many months earlier. I was passionate about doing something to stem the mental health pandemic raging silently through our nation, and what we offered at our gym truly changed lives.

I will never forget the many hundreds of people who walked through our door. Everyone had their own story to tell, each of them unique, but also very familiar.

I met Brad the first time he walked into the gym. He was an accounting professional, but he was shaggy and unshaven, and carried nearly double the weight called for by his slight frame. He wore the gloomy expression of someone carrying the world's problems on their shoulders, and he made fun of himself, telling us he was lazy. Eventually he opened up, sharing his history of depression and how he had reached the point where he was sick and tired of feeling that way. He hadn't stepped inside a gym in over twenty years and was apprehensive, but he was also determined. He felt there was no other choice and I knew the feeling. We set him up with a meal plan, some exercises for his mindset and he was back the following day for his first training session.

Stuart was his trainer and he hated on Stuart big time at the beginning. Those sessions are hard work, but he returned every day like clockwork. Over the following weeks, we saw a change in his demeanour as his energy levels increased and he became much more positive. In one of our follow-up sessions he revealed he'd only grown his beard to cover his double chin, and it was his goal to shave it off. "What a great thing to aim for," I encouraged, and he promised me I could have the glory of shaving it off when the time came.

Brad managed to lose a whopping 48kg. To celebrate we organised a fundraising evening so we could shave his beard off and raise money for Beyond Blue. It was so inspiring, but the best part was seeing the incredible man who had been hiding beneath the beard. He was a confident, happy and good-looking person.

Near the end of the evening his wife came over to thank me for everything we'd done. I explained to her it was all Brad's determination and not us, but she went on to explain, "You don't understand how grateful the kids and I are. Before he came to you, he was suicidal. I would often drive home and be scared I might find him hanging in the lounge room." It hit me in that moment how many people were living with the exact same fears as those that had haunted me. We all think we are alone, but that's not true. We are never alone. Holding her in a warm embrace, my face burst into a huge smile that crinkled my eyes until they prickled with tears. The amazing feeling of making a difference, not only to Brad's life, but also to his beautiful wife and children, was incredibly rewarding.

Every day I was reminded that helping others is one of the most powerful ways to help yourself. Our clients were learning from us, but we were also learning from them. Hearing their stories gave me a fresh perspective on the journey we'd been through over the last year or so; a journey that wasn't over yet. Yes, it was shocking and tumultuous, but some of the people who came to the gym were caught in paralysing situations for many, many years before they'd summoned the courage to take control over their lives. It made me proud we didn't buckle when things got tough. Sure, there were times when I was at a complete loss about what to do next; days when I felt I couldn't go on; nights when I crawled into bed completely deflated. But I noticed something inside me would reset each night. No matter how bad things got, I rose every morning with a fragment of belief and a scrap of determination. It might not have been much, but it was enough to get me through the darkest times.

We had the gym for a year. It was inspiring but exhausting. I could see the fatigue in Stuart's face every night, and we rarely relaxed. There was still a long way to go in supporting Sophie through the upcoming court case, so when someone made an offer to buy the business, it was a perfect reason to pause and take stock. Early on a crisp winter morning, Stuart and I took a rare walk together along the nearby beach. "It's been the most amazing journey and I know one day we are going to do so much more to help other people and make a positive difference to mental health, but our time to continue isn't now," I said. "We have Sophie to think of and we must get her through the court case and out the other side." He was in complete agreement, so we decided to accept the offer.

Chapter 15
The Beginning of the End

After waiting and wondering for more than eighteen months, we were contacted out of the blue and given a trial date in October, approximately three months away. I thought the court case would signal an end to our journey; the clouds hanging over us would lift, justice would be served and the sun would rise on a brand new day. But life is rarely like that ...

It was spring, and the lengthening days spelt the end of a wet and grey winter. As the date neared, I could feel the tension around our home intensify. None of us knew what to expect. The prosecutor's office booked our flights for the Sunday before the trial, which was due to start on the Tuesday. The prosecutor would meet us on Monday to run through the final details.

Sophie now had a boyfriend. They'd been together for about ten months, and when I met Zac I was so pleased to discover he had many of Stuart's qualities. He was calm and supportive, and their friendship was growing into a beautiful, trusting and respectful relationship. I could see he loved Sophie for who she was without judgement or expectation. I wondered how different things might have been if Stuart wasn't in my life at just the right time to provide Sophie with such a fine example of the sort of man she deserved. Zac was making the trip with us, determined to support Sophie through whatever was to come.

On the Saturday night before we left, Stuart and I decided to give Sophie and Zac some space at home, so we arranged to meet with close friends for dinner in the city. We rarely saw this couple because they lived on a farm several hours away, but we always had so much fun and the most interesting conversations about the science of crop farming. I'm a city girl and that stuff fascinates me. The drinks flowed for several hours and our laughter got louder. In the middle of some playful banter I turned to draw Stuart into the debate, but was shocked to see him slumped in his chair.

"Stuart!" I jumped and rushed to his side. As I lifted his head I could see his face was grey and his eyes were unfocused. Suddenly his body was shaking and twitching. "Stuart," I screamed again, trying to steady him in the chair.

"What, what?" he responded croakily, clearly confused and turning his head from side to side trying to find the source of my voice.

"You just passed out," I told him, but before I could say more, his eyes rolled back in his head. "No! Stuart, stay with me." His face contorted into a rigid grimace, as if he was under immense strain, and his body shook violently again. Desperate to get him safely onto the floor, I reached one arm under his legs and the other around his back, struggling to hold his shaking body. My friends were in shock, frantically pushing their chairs back and trying to get around the table to help, but before they could reach us I mustered all my strength and lifted Stuart's tall frame out of the chair and onto the floor. The shaking continued and I screamed out, "Call an ambulance, quick, he needs an ambulance."

As I rolled him onto his side, the shaking eased but he was ghostly pale. I leaned over to check his breathing and he began to come around. Confused and unaware of his surroundings, he then vomited. I didn't know what to do and kept looking desperately around for the paramedics. Our friends helped me to stay calm, and at long last the paramedics were at our side. We stepped back so they could complete their checks, then they put Stuart on a stretcher and we followed them to the ambulance. I was able to travel in the ambulance with Stuart, and by the time we got to the hospital he was more alert and able to speak. He kept downplaying the incident, saying he was okay and probably just drank too much. All the while he was concerned about getting home so we could make the flight to Sophie's trial the next day.

He was seen fairly quickly and the doctor on duty said he needed some tests, but being a Saturday night, it would take some time. Stuart begged them to let him go, promising he would organise to get the tests as soon as he could. I was frightened something was seriously wrong. Over the last few months, Stuart had been complaining of headaches and sleeping more than usual. Tiredness was something we'd been living with for over two years, and with the distraction of the pending trial, I hadn't thought much about it, but now I burst into tears as I pleaded with him; "You need to listen to what I have to say. I am petrified something is wrong. Last night scared the shit out of me!" The emotions from watching my husband lose consciousness and experience seizures were spilling over, and I was almost hysterical. "You are our rock. We cannot survive if something happens to you. I need you to hear what I'm saying and I need you to promise me you'll put your health first. Something is wrong and we need to get it looked at."

"I promise I will," Stuart grabbed my hands trying to calm me down, "but right now Sophie is our priority and we need to get home so we can get on that plane."

We arrived home at 7am. Sophie was up, and when we walked through the door she immediately sensed something was wrong. "Where have you guys been?" she asked.

To avoid stressing her further I said, "We had a bit too much to drink last night. Dad had a funny spell, so we took him to the hospital to get it checked out. He is not feeling well, and when we get back from the trial we'll get some tests done to make sure everything is fine."

Stuart rested in bed while I whipped around the house doing last-minute chores before we were off, heading into the unknown, hoping Sophie would find the justice she rightly deserved.

⁓

My dad met us as we dragged our suitcases out of the airport. His face reflected my own apprehension and concern. I wished we were arriving for a different reason. We'd all been dealing with so much, putting our lives on hold while we faced one test after another. I didn't like seeing the toll it was taking on my dad, but we were a family, all in this together, and I felt great comfort as I snuggled into his arms.

We spent the afternoon settling into Dad's home, but by early evening Stuart was struggling with a bad headache and was still nowhere near his usual self. Dad suggested he go to the hospital after the big football match we'd planned to watch on TV, but when Stuart said, "No, I need to go now," I was shocked. He was a determined man, rarely showing any sign of pain or illness. This wasn't good.

I quickly gathered my things and tried to remain upbeat with Sophie. "It's okay, honey, we'll get him checked out and it will all be fine. You relax and watch the game. We'll be back before you know it."

Sophie gave Stuart a long hug and whispered in his ear, "Three squeezes, Dad."

Stuart held her close for a moment; "Four back, honey." His voice cracked with emotion and I felt a twinge of alarm to see him so shaken.

In the car Stuart told me he didn't know if he could take the stand at the trial feeling the way he did, and he was worried about letting Sophie down. He hoped the doctors might be able to do something to help him get through the next few days. At the hospital he went through the same checks he'd had less than twenty-four hours earlier. The doctor explained that Stuart's pupils were uneven, indicating the need to order a CT scan to check for any bleeds on the brain. My God, it *was* serious! After another hour or so of waiting, the doctor returned with good news; the CT scan was all clear. "But it's only a first step, Stuart. I want you to have an MRI, which will assure us there's nothing more nasty going on." Stuart was resistant to staying any longer at the hospital. He explained to the doctor why we were in town and how important it was to be able to perform his role as a witness at the trial.

The doctor was very understanding, but told us the seizure Stuart experienced would leave him feeling extremely fatigued and vague for several days. "It's an enormous strain on your brain and your body, and under any normal circumstances we would strongly advise you to have complete rest. Given your situation, I can see that's not going to happen." The doctor decided to give Stuart a drug therapy to basically reset his body. "It's a bit like pressing 'control, ALT, delete' on your computer," he said. It would knock him out for several hours, but he should wake feeling much better. The doctor agreed to let Stuart go home when he woke from the therapy, on the condition he got an MRI without delay when we flew home at the end of the week.

I went back to Dad's to get some sleep. I felt an aching exhaustion, as if I'd been competing in one of those ultramarathons where the competitors must run all night, navigating their way through the wilderness in the dark with no assistance. My brain was tired and my body was sore. I fell asleep before my head hit the pillow, but was woken a short time later by the phone – Stuart was ready to come home. I dragged my clothes on and crept out of the house, trying not to disturb the others. It was only 1am, and while Stuart and I were going to be completely drained before we even stepped into the courtroom, I didn't want Sophie to feel sleep-deprived on top of the anxiety I knew she was carrying.

Stuart was still groggy and unsteady on his feet, but he said he felt better. We went straight home and fell into bed, desperate to sleep for a few more hours before we met with the prosecutor later in the morning.

Do you know the feeling of looking forward to something and dreading it at the same time? That's how I'd been feeling about the trial for two years. It was something I didn't want to face, but I knew we needed to meet it head-on if we were to ever reach the other side. Tension had been mounting like the pressure of an unreleased breath, and I was impatient for this moment to arrive. Once it did, I just wanted it to be over.

Monday would involve only a meeting with the prosecutor, which for us was extremely important. Having no idea what to expect at the trial, I assumed the meeting would prepare us for what we would face over the following two days. The Monday was a public holiday, but the city streets were full of traffic as we made our way into town. I could hear Dad speaking with the taxi driver who explained there was some sort of environmental protest underway. Apparently a group of protestors had chained themselves to a big barrel in the middle of an intersection. Police were everywhere, trying to keep the traffic moving, but it was a thankless task. With horns blaring all around, our taxi driver off-loaded us a few blocks early and we walked. I was oblivious to the chaos, focused only on getting to our destination.

The meeting with the prosecutor I hoped would offer some clarity, merely served to heighten my anxiety. We were called into the interview room one at a time, with Sophie going first. The rest of us sat for a long time in the drab waiting room making the occasional remark or joke to keep ourselves awake. I was called in next. I passed Sophie on her way out of the room, but her expression was unreadable. As I sat down at the table I tried to explain Stuart's shaky state of health, but there was no sign of interest and no compassion. The prosecutor fired questions at me that seemed to come from nowhere; things about our family from the years when Sophie was very young. When I asked why, I was told dismissively, "I cannot give you any details. I will ask the questions here, not you."

That condescending tone is one I've struggled to handle all my life. I'm sure it harks back to my mother, triggering the little girl in me who immediately doubts herself and loses all confidence. I was shocked at the heartlessness of the process. The woman I am now would no longer tolerate such unnecessary disrespect for a fellow human, but back then I was powerless in the face of such disdain. I sat there and did as I was told, feeling small and insignificant and completely humiliated. I left the room confused and disheartened. Was this the team who were supposedly representing Sophie's case tomorrow? I felt a bleak sense of foreboding about the trial.

Chapter 16
The Lion's Den

The trial would run for two days. Waking early on the first morning, I flitted nervously between Sophie and Stuart, unsure which of them concerned me most. I was grateful Sophie had Zac to lean on, and after checking in with her a few times, she told me to give her space. While I was worried, I was also extremely proud of her. She'd worked hard with her psychologist to prepare for this day. She was ready to stand up and reveal the truth of her childhood, making it clear to her father she remembered everything and was no longer prepared to remain silent about the wrongs done to her.

Her godparents Macy and Tim had flown in to support us, and knowing me well, Macy said, "Okay, darl, what do we need to do?" I rambled through a chaotic list of tasks that were whirling through my head, knowing my friend's steady hand would make light of it all. "You go and get ready while I get everyone fed," she ordered, and I readily complied, happy for a little time to myself.

When I returned to the kitchen I declined Macy's offer of breakfast, unable to stomach any food. I would have killed for a real coffee, but Dad didn't have anything but the instant type, and I wasn't that desperate. I'd ordered a large taxi the night before and we waited quietly on the sidewalk. It reminded me of the day of my mother's funeral when I'd stood in the same spot before we drove to the service. For a moment I wished she was there with us. For all her faults, she had a way of keeping the energy high, and in that moment I really needed something to distract me from my ominous thoughts. There was no happy ending in the ruminations circling through my mind.

Following the same route as the day before, I was once again oblivious to my surroundings. We were seven people, but each of us seemed lost in our own thoughts. The only conversation was some small talk between Dad and the taxi driver. On arrival at the courthouse we were taken to a waiting area. While it would be possible for us to sit in the courtroom later, Sophie, Stuart and I were required to wait until after we appeared as witnesses.

Sophie was called first. Prior to the trial the judge had ruled her to be a vulnerable witness, which meant she could take the stand from another room via video, with a woman from the child victim support group sitting beside her. The court would be closed and only the essential court members would hear her testimony. I was relieved. It's hard enough having to relive such confronting experiences in front of complete strangers, but worse to have the perpetrator sitting right there in the room with you.

As she stood, I jumped up and hugged her tight. "You are amazingly strong, baby. You've got this! Speak the truth and set it free." My words were confident, but deep down I was trembling. Watching her diminutive figure disappear down the corridor was like watching a martyr being led into an arena to face a pack of wild animals, knowing they would drag her through her living nightmares and make vicious attacks on her memories. But she went willingly, prepared to sacrifice her dignity in the pursuit of what she believed was right.

Then we waited. Time dragged cruelly until suddenly a door banged open and I heard a gut-wrenching wail. It was Sophie running out of the witness room where she was giving her testimony. She leaned against the wall sobbing hysterically. I leapt out of my chair and dashed toward her, but the supporter had her arm around Sophie's heaving shoulders and gently shook her head at me, miming that it was alright. As the woman gently led Sophie back into the witness room, I turned away and found Zac standing right behind me. I sank into his arms, knowing we were all feeling tormented by our inability to soothe Sophie's pain. It was torture!

The trial continued into the afternoon before Sophie was released. When she came out of the witness room, she ran straight into Zac's arms. The hardest part was done and her relief was obvious. Now Stuart and I would be called to give our testimony.

I was called first. I turned to Stuart and he gave me the biggest hug. "Honey, you've got this," he reassured me. My legs were trembling as I walked into the court room. I was too nervous to look around at all the people; the jury, the judge, the lawyers or even my dad. I especially didn't want to make eye contact with Sophie's father; the one person who no longer merited a moment of my precious time on this earth. As I stood holding up my hand to swear on the Bible, my eyes were unseeing and my heart raced. All I heard were the words in my head; *Just breathe and tell the truth.*

I was completely unprepared for the barrage of questions thrown at me. I was almost in tears when I walked out of the court room thirty minutes later. I went straight over to Stuart and let him wrap me up in his arms. I was relieved it was over, but before I could utter a word, his name was called. I could see he still felt ill, so I cupped his face in my hands and looked straight into his eyes. "Honey, just tell the truth and do your best. That is all we can do. I love you, honey. You've got this."

Not ten minutes passed before Stuart returned looking wretched. He sat back beside me and we held hands for a moment without speaking.

"My mind was so foggy," he finally revealed. "I couldn't remember things properly. I don't know, maybe I stuffed it up." It made me angry to think we were so badly prepared for such a significant event. I expected we would be more supported, but maybe this was normal? I thought the system was supposed to stand up for our vulnerable young people, but instead it forced those who spoke up to endure a process that seemed devoid of care and compassion. We'd walked into a lion's den with no protection. Sure, justice means all parties have rights, but I couldn't see how justice would be served when the prosecution team didn't even verify important details. They hadn't chased up potential witnesses such as Dr Rama, other family members, or the friends who spent time with us during periods that were crucial to Sophie's statement. The pretext phone call, which had caused her so much heartache, was never mentioned. At a crucial point in the case the prosecutor specifically stated Sophie had not been diagnosed with PTSD, which was clearly wrong. This series of mistakes and missteps would cost dearly in the end.

I've never read the trial transcript and I never want to. It might sound like I am denying reality, but there is a sanity in protecting your mind from the things you cannot control. And what happens inside a courtroom is something you cannot control.

After two years of waiting, worrying and wondering how the final act would play out, I sat in the courtroom on the second day listening as the prosecutor, barrister and judge entered into a long discussion about a technicality of law. A hard ball of fear formed in my stomach. The jury were removed from the courtroom while the issue was explored. The barrister suggested the jury would not have the required knowledge to determine if memories of trauma, suffered when Sophie was very young, could resurface at the age of sixteen. He proposed that, without guidance from a psychiatrist experienced in sexual abuse memories, the jury would be unable to come to a conclusion in this case. The judge was clearly swayed by the argument, and the prosecutor was unable to successfully influence him otherwise. It was like watching a collision unfold in slow motion and being unable to do anything to stop it. My body was paralysed even as my mind rushed in to avert the carnage. *No!* was the silent scream from every cell in my body when I heard the judge direct the jury to return a finding of not guilty, a cruel command that robbed them of their opportunity to weigh up the details of the actual case presented to them. The judge decided the prosecutor should have called an expert in what he labelled 'the science of memory', and having failed to do so, the judge determined the prosecution's case to be fatally flawed. My head began to spin and I felt a sudden jolt of pain as the judge brought his hammer down on my world. The loud 'crack' seemed to echo forever.

~

I couldn't move. I was in shock. *Why wasn't someone fixing this? If the judge wanted another expert to be called, why couldn't they just do it? Why was everyone walking away as if it was the end of an ordinary office meeting? This was important. It was about people's lives. It was about our lives!*

My family had to drag me out of the courtroom and we stood in the corridor in stunned silence, unsure what to do next. Zac and Sophie had remained outside, so they didn't hear the outcome. She would want an explanation. *I* wanted an explanation. I wanted to know how this could happen. How could I tell Sophie that all her heartache and courage was for nothing? Dad and Stuart finally turned towards the exit, but I refused to leave. I was determined to find someone who could explain how this happened. Dad grabbed my arm, saying sternly, "Rose, we have to go."

Stuart grabbed Dad's arm telling him, "Leave her alone. She needs to do this." We were all shaken and confused, and our emotions were spilling over uncontrollably.

The prosecutor and assistant finally came out through the court-room doors, still wearing their cloaks. "You have to do something," I demanded.

"Rose, there is nothing we can do." The prosecutor raised a hand in front of my face as if to silence me.

"What do you mean there is nothing you can do?" I felt like the prosecution team had let us down and I was so angry.

"As I said, there is nothing we can do."

"What, just like that?"

"Yes."

"How dare you? How fucking dare you? You have destroyed my family. You have torn my entire family apart," I screamed.

"Rose, you need to calm down. You can call the office tomorrow if you wish to discuss it," and with that they turned and walked away. I never saw them again, but Sophie tried to find out more and was told the same thing; nothing could be done. "You need to get on with your life," they told her. It was heartless.

Chapter 17
The Aftermath

Our travel home was sombre. I gave Dad a long hug before we parted ways at the airport. We had all calmed down, but it was obvious everyone was wary of opening up a discussion about the trial. The emotions were too raw and none of us had come to terms with what we'd experienced in the last few days.

I was consumed by rage. I couldn't sleep. I couldn't concentrate on anything. I questioned the universe – *Why is this happening to us?* I beat myself up for my naivety, for expecting that speaking the truth would bring justice. I was angry at the legal professionals in whom we'd placed our faith and trust. I was tormented by anxiety and worried how it would affect Sophie. Laying herself bare to strangers and being dismissed so cruelly must have felt like being raped all over again. After everything it took to get here, would this push her back to the edge of the cliff? Stuart kept telling me he felt guilty for not being at his best. He worried it was his fault. I felt the same sense of responsibility, but I knew the outcome was not our fault, which made it even more frustrating.

My anxiety returned and was completely out of control. I had to do something to fix this. I searched the internet for options. After hours scrolling through legal sites and support groups, I discovered there was no avenue for a victim to appeal a trial decision. Those rights existed only for the person charged with the crime. It deepened my anger and my frustration. Surely there was a way to correct the wrong done to my daughter. My only avenue seemed to be a direct appeal to the Attorney-General. Once more I wrote a letter, pouring my heart out in the hope that a person with influence could help us. I detailed what I thought were the failings of Sophie's case and asked for it to be reviewed. I expressed my strong concern that our legal system could allow a procedural matter to thwart justice. Whether or not the letter would fall on deaf ears, I had to send it. I couldn't leave any stone unturned.

It wasn't just about Sophie; it was about every soul who put their faith in any system. Over the last two and a half years I'd been an unwilling witness to what went on behind the curtain in our hospitals, mental health services, police and legal system. I'd known nothing of the silent struggles faced by millions of my fellow Australians every day, nor of the unceasing demands placed on millions more who were trying to ease their pain. Before my daughter slid into her trauma, I was living in blissful ignorance, but my ignorance blinded me to the bleak landscape lying right at my door. The more I wandered through it trying to navigate a way out for my family, the more I saw its pitfalls. We met admirable people, but we also stumbled in the face of heartless barriers. I didn't only want to help Sophie, I wanted to leave a kinder and more compassionate path for others to follow. I wish we were the last to travel this road, but the sad fact is, we won't be. In 2018, the year before Sophie's trial, more than 3,000 children in Australia were sexually assaulted by a family member.**

I received a letter back nearly seven weeks later and it reinforced what I'd already been told; there was nothing anyone could do about the outcome of Sophie's trial. By the time the letter arrived, I barely cared. We were focused on a new heartbreaking drama that had crept silently into our lives while we were looking the other way.

~

When we arrived home from the trial, I made appointments for Stuart to get an MRI and see our doctor. We'd promised the hospital medics we'd do it immediately, and after watching how scattered Stuart was during the trial, there was no way we could leave it any longer. "Nothing is wrong with me," he said angrily, "I don't know why you are insisting on getting this done. It's a waste of time and money." I desperately wanted to believe him, but I had a nagging feeling all was not well. I'd been focused on Sophie for such a long time, but after he had the seizure I recognised subtle changes in Stuart's personality. He was short-tempered and impatient – a trait I'd not seen in him before. The foggy mind he'd complained of during the trial was not new. He'd been forgetful and a little absent for many months before his seizure. I think I'd subconsciously put it down to the immense stress we'd all been under for the last few years. Heaven knows I'd been much more irritable and mindless myself, but I was concerned this was something more sinister.

"Honey, if you are okay that's great, but we can't ignore the advice. Let's get it checked out so we can at least have peace of mind," I encouraged him.

The following day he called me around lunchtime saying, "The MRI is done, so can we drop it now?"

Later that afternoon I got a call from the centre; "Ma'am, we've contacted your husband because we would like him to come back for a contrast MRI. We inject dye into the blood stream to get a better view of the area. He said he is too busy with work for the rest of today and tomorrow, however we strongly recommend he doesn't delay."

My heart was racing fast and I immediately rang Stuart. "Honey, you need to go back there."

"Rose, I'm too busy for this shit. I have a meeting this afternoon and meetings all morning tomorrow. It'll have to wait."

"No, it can't wait. This is your health we are talking about."

"I'm fine. This is just another way for them to make money. They scare you so you will fork out for more tests. I am not talking about it any longer. I have to go."

As I tried to focus on finishing my work, I felt the same mental battle I'd faced every day during Sophie's worst phases. My unease about Stuart's health, on top of the resentment I was still carrying from Sophie's trial, was a massive drain on my energy. I found it hard to concentrate and I rushed through my meetings. When I arrived home I raised it again, but Stuart wouldn't budge. He made it very clear he was extremely busy and stressed at work. He said he would go on Friday to get the contrast MRI done, "If I have time."

After he went to bed I sat up and searched the internet for possible explanations of his symptoms. Like most people who consult Dr Google, the more I looked, the more anxious I became. I shut my computer and sent my boss a text message advising him I would be late the next day because I needed to attend a medical appointment with my husband.

No more regrets, I told myself as I lay down to sleep.

The alarm went off at the usual time of 4:30am and Stuart went straight to the shower. I got up and walked into the ensuite, apprehensive about how to raise it with him again. In fact, I was already trembling as I said quietly, "Honey, you need to go and get the second MRI done this morning."

"Rose, I told you I'm not doing it today," he replied firmly from the shower.

"No. Something is wrong and you must do it this morning. If I have learnt anything over the past few years, it's to listen to the warning signs and act fast, no matter what it is. I would do anything to go back and protect Sophie, but I can't. I don't want to live with any more regrets. What if you suffered another seizure on your way to work? I would never be able to live with myself. I've already sent my boss a message to tell him I won't be in, so if you insist on going to work, I will drive you then I'll take you to the centre for the scan when they open." I was in full negotiation mode, talking fast and leaving no space for him to object.

"You are not going to drive me into work and sit there. It's a worksite full of tradies. I'm not going to have my wife babysitting me."

"Fine, I will sit outside in the car. I'm not budging. You can either call your work and tell them you're not coming in this morning, or I'll drive you there and wait in the car. What's it going to be?" He was silent for a long time and I waited nervously for his decision.

"Okay, you win. I'll call work. I can't believe you're doing this to me." He was stubbornly quiet for the next few hours, but that was fine. I could handle his annoyance much better than I could handle another day of worry and uncertainty.

The moment the clock hit 8:30am I called the centre and they told me to bring him straight in. As I sat in the waiting room, I pondered the sense of déjà vu teasing my mind. I'd sat in too many of these anonymous rooms with their harsh lights and their hard seats waiting anxiously for one or another medical person to tell me what was wrong with my daughter. Now I was doing the same for my husband. It seemed absurd. This stuff doesn't even happen in movies. I wondered how my life would sound to a stranger if I tried to describe the last few years. I doubted anyone would believe me. Some days I hardly believed it myself.

We'd have to wait until the next day for the results. I was scheduled to travel interstate with some of my staff and I was out of bed at 3am to catch the first flight. It was a full day of important meetings so I didn't get a chance to speak with Stuart until I was waiting at the airport for my return flight, around 4:30pm. He told me our doctor had rung and he'd been in to see him. "What did he say," I asked anxiously.

"Rose, it's all okay. I'll explain it when you get home. How did your meetings go?" he asked, smoothly changing the subject. I was relieved he was alright. He sounded fine and I was happy to have some time to sit and chat with him after the crazy week.

I arrived home at 10pm to find the house abuzz with activity. Sophie and Zac had cooked a lovely dinner for Stuart and were cleaning up when I walked in. They were smiling and laughing and I was pleased to see Sophie looking so relaxed this soon after the trial. Maybe she was dealing with it better than me. I sat with them for a while catching up on their day, and as Stuart said goodnight to the kids, I finished emptying my briefcase and followed him into our bedroom.

Stuart was standing quite still, looking absently at the bed. "Honey, what is it?" I asked. When he turned to face me, he was pale and his eyes glistened with tears.

"I saw the doctor today."

"Yes, but I thought everything was okay. What happened?"

"I didn't want to tell you over the phone … I have a brain tumour."

No! I couldn't believe what I was hearing. *Not that, not now.* I threw myself against him. This man who'd stood steady in the face of our turmoil, who'd dragged us out of the darkest places; I thought he was invincible. I never imagined anything could break him, but here he was in tears, facing his own dark test. *How could this be happening?*

We lay in each other's arms talking, crying and hugging for hours. All the unrest of the last few weeks was swept from my mind. My exhaustion evaporated as I drank in every tender moment beside my precious man. The sound of his voice, the smell of his skin, the pressure of his body entwined with mine; I never wanted the night to end. I didn't want to fall asleep and be forced to wake back into a world where a sinister new threat waited to menace us. We were so close to a new dawn, but now I realised the clouds had never left us.

In the morning we woke to a difficult situation; how to tell Sophie and Stuart's sons what was happening with their dad. Stuart was terrified about telling them, not wanting to cause more distress, but they were all adults and they needed to know. I brought him a coffee in bed, and not long afterward Sophie came bounding down the stairs and into our room. Her mood had lifted dramatically in the last few days, which made it even harder.

With one glance she could sense something was wrong, and she stopped in her tracks. "Dad, what is it?"

Stuart gestured for her to sit beside him on the bed. "Remember when I went to the hospital just before the trial?" She nodded slowly. "Well, I had some tests and I saw the doctor yesterday." He paused, unable to look her in the eye. "Honey, he told me I've got a brain tumour."

Sophie flung her arms around Stuart's shoulders and buried her face against his neck. Her body heaved with sobs and her muffled groans ascended quickly into despairing cries; "No! Please no. Not my dad. I can't lose you now. I finally have a father who really loves me – and now this? Please, no, Dad, please don't ever leave me." It was heartbreaking to stand by and watch these two souls, whose deep love for each other had been strengthened by the painful road we'd recently travelled, once again locked together in pain.

Stuart's sons didn't live locally, so he faced the even more difficult task of having to break his news to them over the phone. His eldest son lived and worked in Europe and he immediately wanted to fly home, but Stuart convinced him not to make a rash decision. He was due holidays in about a month's time and said he would make arrangements to come back to Australia then to see his dad. It was something wonderful for Stuart to look forward to; the rare event of having his sons together in one place. If only it was being planned under better circumstances.

We told our closest friends about Stuart's diagnosis and I noticed a strange thing. I'd avoided telling even my dearest and most trusted friends about the crisis we faced with Sophie until many months had passed. I wondered at the difference. Was it because of the stigma mental health carries in our society that I'd stayed quiet? It certainly took me a long time to understand Sophie's situation, and explaining it to anyone else felt impossible in the beginning. Once I accepted it and began telling friends, I discovered they would respond in one of two ways: by offering their total and unquestioning support, or by shutting me down and pulling away. It made me cautious about opening up, except with those closest to me. Most of the time I would simply put on a brave face, but there was no such withdrawal from anyone who heard about Stuart's brain tumour. It made me aware how deeply affected we are by societal prejudice. Most of the time we don't even notice how much influence these unconscious viewpoints have over our decisions. Mental health, sexual abuse, youth suicide and family trauma are still largely considered taboo subjects, and many people carry their burdens in silence. I'd discovered the hard way that silence was dangerous. Only the truth can heal.

Chapter 18
On the Edge Again

The neurosurgeon turned his computer around so we could see Stuart's brain scans. He pointed to the tumour in Stuart's right frontal lobe. "It needs to come out," he said casually, explaining how it was causing the seizures. "The tumour is in the best location to operate and it is quite an easy surgery." I couldn't believe any brain surgery was easy, but I was glad to hear that. The surgeon remarked on Stuart's obvious strength and fitness, and reassured us it would be an advantage when facing surgery. I felt myself relax a bit as the two of them chatted about gyms and strength training for a few moments; a couple of laidback guys discussing a shared interest. But when the surgeon nonchalantly moved back to describing the surgery and how they would cut through Stuart's skull, I could feel my whole body tense up. While the thought of that was daunting enough, it was his warning as he handed me a prescription for antiseizure medication that really frightened me. "I want you to ring me any time, day or night, if he starts to have another seizure. It's a life-threatening condition and time is of the essence." He turned to Stuart and his manner was suddenly very serious. "If you have another seizure we need to get you in for surgery immediately. It can be a matter of life or death."

Another life or death scenario. There was no pause between the journey we'd taken with Sophie and the one we were beginning for Stuart. They overlapped in a way that felt cruel and unfair. Instead of relaxing after the long-awaited trial, we were being sucked into the vortex of a new drama just as uncertain and scary as the one that had ruled our lives for the last few years.

～

We waited two weeks until Stuart could have his surgery, and during that time he was not allowed to work. The risk of another seizure was too high for him to drive a car or be around large construction equipment. Sophie and I spent as much time with him as possible, knowing the long days stuck in an empty house made him feel useless and frustrated. I raced home each day with the same trepidation I'd felt when Sophie was home alone. While Stuart's medical condition seemed to have a clear-cut solution, the memory of his seizure was still fresh in my mind, and I held my breath whenever I returned to the house, not knowing what I would find.

Anxiety had its claws in me again. It's a crazy feeling – like being infected with a virus that works you into a frenzy and steals away any sensible thoughts. I was running on adrenalin, exhausted but unable to slow down or relax. I was constantly looking for something to do, then feeling completely overwhelmed by even the smallest task. My mind imagined all sorts of scenarios, and none of them were good.

Stuart tried hard to remain positive and strong, but the thought of someone cutting open his skull and digging around in his brain terrified him. We had some agonising conversations. When he raised the possibility of death I wanted to stop him, but I could see he needed to say it out loud. "I can't help but think about the possibility I won't make it through this."

I hugged him tight, holding back my tears. "Honey, I know how easy it is to get caught up in the worst-case scenario, especially with all the time on your hands to think and worry, but it's not an option." I lifted my head and stared at him hard, tears now flowing freely, "We've got too much living left to do together."

I had a very emotional conversation with Sophie. From the moment Stuart told me about his tumour, we were completely focused on how we were going to get through it. However, Sophie's journey felt unfinished and I wondered whether she was really okay. We hadn't talked about the trial at all, and while my anger about how it ended faded fast when I discovered my husband was in danger, my worry about Sophie was ever-present. When Zac was talking to Stuart one night, I climbed the stairs to Sophie's bedroom. "How are you going, sweetie?" I asked.

"Oh, Mum, I'm so worried about Dad. I can't believe this is happening to him. He's the last person I ever expected to have something so horrible happen. Are you alright?"

I walked over and sat next to her on the bed. "I'm just focusing on getting him through. Thank you so much for everything you're doing. It's going to turn out fine. We have to believe that."

She hugged me and we sat in silence for a moment. Then I tentatively asked her, "How are you feeling about the trial and everything that happened? I don't want you to think you can't talk to me about it."

She had been bravely controlling her emotions, but now they rose to the surface and tears welled in her eyes. "Mum, I was in total shock at the beginning. I felt so betrayed that I had to relive it all, only for him to get off on a technicality. The injustice of it hurts so much at times and my heart physically aches." As she cried I held her against my body, wishing I could take her pain away. When she settled, she lifted her head and looked at me with glistening eyes. "Now I understand why everyone kept saying I needed to go through this process. It feels like I can begin to heal. I'm proud of myself for speaking up. I know it will take time to grieve, but it has made me stronger. I'm ready to put it behind me and move on. I don't want to ruin the rest of my life because of it."

She sat up straight and for a moment she looked defiant and strong, but a shadow crossed her face and she continued, "Then this happens to Dad? He's the last person who deserves it. Mum, you and I have been Dad's priority for so long, now it's time for him to be our priority. The only thing I care about now is Dad. The rest is in the past." My daughter's maturity left me in awe. I realised how far she'd come and how different she was from the girl who, just two years earlier, could find no reason to go on. She'd walked through darkness, placing one foot in front of the other every day, and reached the other side. Maybe it was time to let go of my fears. She was no longer on the edge of a cliff. Yes, she would have bad days like everyone else, but she knew how to get herself through them now. I could learn a lot from her.

⌒

While my anxiety for Sophie abated, I couldn't set aside my concerns for Stuart. There was still too much uncertainty, something that doesn't sit easy with me. Against my better judgement I went back to researching his condition on the internet. I discovered the right frontal lobe of the brain is involved in motor function, problem solving, spontaneity, memory, language, judgement, impulse control, and social and sexual behavior. If the surgery didn't go well, would it change the husband and father we all knew and loved? Could he end up with brain damage? I found myself talking to God or the universe or whatever higher power would listen to me. Some days I protested angrily: *Haven't we been through enough?*

Why are you being so cruel to us? What the hell have we done to deserve this? On other days I tried to bargain: *Please get him through this. I will do anything you want, I promise. Just get my husband through.* Most days I simply asked the question I couldn't answer for myself: *What lesson are you trying to teach me?*

While I couldn't work out what lesson I was supposed to learn from our latest blow, I had learnt some things over those last few years; I was responsible for my own attitude, and letting myself drown in anxiety would help no one. I convinced Stuart to join me in filling out a gratitude diary. Each night we acknowledged the amazing blessings filling our lives. Some days he found it difficult, but he would always identify something. The antiseizure medication was making it difficult for him to read or write, so I wrote for both of us.

I didn't stop there. I'd read about the importance of cleansing negativity from your home and I was prepared to try anything. Convincing Stuart to play along, I bought a sage smudge stick, which we lit and waved around like incense as we wandered through the house. I then circled Stuart with it, almost choking him to death with the amount of smoke floating through the air. God bless him, he was so patient – not really believing in that stuff, but so understanding. He knew I couldn't sit still, and with my new motto of 'no regrets', he also knew I couldn't be diverted from trying any idea if it offered even a whiff of hope.

On the day before he checked into hospital, I stood with electric clippers in hand, ready to shave Stuart's head. We considered going to a barber but Stuart wanted me to do it at home. Determined to honor his wishes, I positioned him on a chair in the kitchen and threw a towel around his shoulders. I'd never done it before, so I circled him nervously, wondering where to start. I had to be extra careful because if I cut him or even nicked his skin, the operation would be postponed until he healed. It was a point of no return. Trying to put him at ease, or maybe to delay a little longer, I suggested we start with a Mohawk. That raised a few chuckles but nothing near the level of laughter and banter that would normally flow between us. My hands were trembling as I took a deep breath and began.

When I finished, I stepped back to survey my work. My heart broke to see my husband this way. The silver hair that contrasted so dramatically with his piercing blue eyes was gone. I saw a man stripped of his vitality and aged by the battle raging within his body. The high doses of antiseizure medication made his eyes dull, but I could still see his fear and doubt reflected there. All I could do was wrap him up in my arms, hoping my belief in him would pass through our embrace and give him strength.

The next day I took him into hospital where they went through the preoperative tests and confirmed him to be fit as a fiddle – except for that damn tumour sitting in his brain! They would prepare him for the following day's procedure and monitor him overnight, but I was able to stay for a few hours. The hospital was modern and had an amazing list of food we could order for dinner. It was restaurant quality and we made a date out of it, trying to keep our minds off what tomorrow might bring.

⌒

Sophie, Zac and I took the day off work and went straight up to the hospital on the morning of the surgery. Stuart was trying hard to remain strong and calm, but I could tell he was anxious. I was too. It helped a lot that Sophie and I were able to accompany him into the preoperative area; a cold and sterile place where staff buzzed to and fro wheeling patients in and out of surgery. We shuffled around, dodging the staff who came to prepare him, trying to crack silly little jokes to conceal our nerves. The anaesthetist came to check him over and put a line in. He asked a ton of questions but he was cool as a cucumber, and why wouldn't he be? It was just a normal day for him.

When it was Stuart's turn to be wheeled into surgery, I didn't want to let him go. The orderly waited patiently while I held on for a few more moments. "You've got this, honey. We'll be here when you come out. Love you more than anything."

As he was wheeled away, I called out, "Three squeezes, honey." There was no way I could let him leave my sight without those special words. They carried not only my undying love, but the love of our whole family.

"Four back, Rosey," his words floated toward me, and I held on to the familiar sound of his voice as Sophie and I watched him disappear.

Chapter 19
The Final Twist

"Stuart is fine." The surgeon's voice on the end of the phone relayed the news I was hoping to hear. I could feel the weight lift from my shoulders as he continued. "The operation went well. We managed to remove all of the tumour. It looks benign, but we will have to wait for pathology to confirm that in a few days. If you go to the intensive care unit in a couple of hours, you'll be able to see him."

Sophie and Zac watched my face intently and could see it was good news. When I hung up we jumped around in joyous celebration, oblivious to the pedestrians trying to get past us on the crowded street. With many hours to wait, we had wandered to the shops near the hospital, trying to distract ourselves while we waited for the call. I messaged Stuart's sons with the good news, knowing they were standing by anxiously on opposite sides of the globe.

Now all we needed to do was to focus on his recovery, then we could return to normal lives, or whatever might pass for normal once we'd assimilated the upheavals life had thrown at us. I knew we could never return to the original trajectory our lives were on three years earlier, but I was sure things would calm down now and we'd be allowed to enjoy the many things we'd missed, such as spontaneous weekends away, our treasured walks along the beach and exploring the world together.

We waited patiently outside the intensive care unit and were finally allowed in. We found Stuart propped up on some pillows, his head wrapped in a thick bandage. Sophie and I looked at each other and giggled as we realised I didn't need to shave his head. They had gone in through his forehead! He was groggy and a little pale, but the nurses told us he was doing well. I was so relieved to see him, and I held his hand while we talked quietly. "You're here, honey. You made it."

The neurosurgeon told us Stuart would be in hospital for seven days before he could come home. I spent all the hours I could visiting him, eating meals with him and helping him to shower. A few days later we received confirmation that the tumour was benign. It was wonderful news, but even though I felt we'd turned a corner, I noticed Stuart wasn't his normal self. He was forgetting things and often completely ignored me. I put it down to the fact he'd just been through major surgery and desperately wanted to come home. He hated being in hospital, and he didn't hide his agitation well.

My dad arranged to visit and spend a week with us so he could be at home with Stuart while I went to work. On day five, the doctor on the ward unexpectedly told us Stuart could go home. I was reluctant, as that wasn't what we'd planned. I would have to go to work the next day and Dad hadn't yet arrived. I didn't want to leave Stuart alone on his first day home, and I had a niggling feeling the doctors were rushing the decision. But Stuart begged me to take him home and I knew he badly wanted to get out of there, so I agreed.

The next day, a Monday morning, I set him up in the lounge room with everything he might need or want for the day before I kissed him goodbye and headed off to work. I called him several times during the day to put my mind at ease. It wasn't abnormal for us to call each other whenever we had something interesting or important to share. It was one of our little pleasures, a sign of how close we were that we hated going a day without hearing each other's voices, but during the last phone call late in the afternoon Stuart became aggressive, yelling at me over a trivial matter. It was completely out of character and it made me uneasy. I raced straight home and found him sitting on the couch, seemingly fine, but as we went about our normal evening routine, I knew something wasn't right. My husband was not himself; in fact I was a little scared of him. One moment I would catch him staring at me blankly, and the next he would ignore me completely. Then he would abruptly come to and snap at me.

"Stuart, are you alright? Are you feeling okay?" I asked.

"Yes I'm fine. Get off my case, would you?"

Unsure what to do, I suggested he take a shower. He was still in his pyjamas from the night before and he would need my assistance. He refused, once more dismissing me gruffly. I was exhausted and needed some sleep, so I suggested he come to bed. He declined, saying he wanted to sit up for a while longer and would come to bed soon. I was conscious my anxiety combined with my tiredness could be making me sound edgy, so I decided not to hassle him any further and went off to bed.

I woke with a fright, another nightmare shaking me from my sleep. Stuart wasn't in bed next to me and the clock revealed it was almost midnight. I could hear the faint sound of the TV and hurried out to the lounge room. Stuart was sitting on the couch staring at his phone in his hand.

"Stuart, honey, what are you doing?" He raised his blue eyes to mine, but he didn't respond.

"Honey, are you okay?" He seemed unable to speak, but there was desperation in his eyes, a silent appeal for help.

"Oh no, something's wrong. Honey, please smile for me," I pleaded, as I put my hands to his face. Maybe it was a stroke. He gave no response at all.

I glanced at his phone but the battery was dead. Had he been trapped here alone staring at the phone while I was sleeping just one room away? My heart thumped hard in my chest and I reached for the surgeon's card, dialling his number with trembling hands. When he answered I spluttered, "I need your help. There's something wrong with Stuart!" He asked me a few questions then told me to check Stuart's pulse. I couldn't find it on his wrist. All I could feel was the wild beat of my own heart. After a few more questions he suggested I put Stuart to bed. I couldn't believe what I was hearing. "No, something is seriously wrong," I disagreed adamantly. "I'm going to call an ambulance." I had to trust my gut instinct that whatever was happening couldn't be ignored.

As I dialled the emergency number, I leant in close to Stuart to reassure him I was getting help. Suddenly I heard a distinct thumping and realised his heart was pumping so hard and fast I could hear it outside of his chest. It was frightening. *Rose, stay calm, you must stay calm*, I kept telling myself even as my own heart raced even faster.

A moment of déjà vu hit me when the woman on the end of the line asked me to say 'now' every time Stuart took a breath. She was calm and reassuring, asking more questions and confirming an ambulance was on the way.

All of a sudden Stuart's head jerked, turning repeatedly to the right. His eyes were begging me to do something but I didn't have any idea where to start. I felt so helpless. "Please, honey, hang in there with me." I begged the woman to stay on the phone with me too. She reassured me she wasn't going anywhere. I just needed to be her eyes and ears and she would tell me what to do. I felt so alone and terrified, sobbing, "He is my life, he is my everything, please, please, please I need him to be okay."

It seemed to take forever, but the paramedics arrived within eleven minutes. As I opened the door to them, I hung up the phone, grateful for the calm woman who had been my lifeline. The paramedics quickly told me Stuart was critical and they would take him to hospital immediately.

When I told them the surgeon wanted him taken to the one where he had the surgery, they explained it was not possible. "He is critical and we have to get him to the nearest major trauma unit. You need to come with us. We cannot let you drive in the state you're in."

I flew into the bedroom and threw on whatever clothes I could find while they got Stuart into the ambulance, then I jumped into the front seat and we took off. The moment we turned onto the main road, the paramedic in the back attending to Stuart signalled for lights and sirens. *Oh my God, this can't be happening!* It was so much more urgent than the ride I'd taken with Sophie so long ago. As the ambulance sped through the streets, I could see flashes as we triggered the red light cameras at every intersection. It felt so surreal.

The ambulance raced into the hospital's emergency entrance and they rushed Stuart into the resuscitation room. I stood at the door watching helplessly while they unclipped him from the gurney to move him to the bed. Right at that moment, his body thrashed so violently that he threw himself off the gurney. Suddenly an alarm was clanging and I could hear the words 'Code Blue' repeating over the loud speaker. People came rushing from every direction but I was frozen, unable to believe the drama unfolding before me could possibly be real.

A softly-spoken woman came up and put her arm around me. She gently steered me into a private waiting room across the hallway. "Can I get you a tea or coffee?" she asked kindly.

"No, thank you," I responded, barely glancing at her. I moved towards a chair to sit down, but I couldn't. I didn't know what to do. I paced back and forth then grabbed my phone and called Stuart's eldest son.

As soon as I heard his voice I burst into tears. "Something is seriously wrong with Dad. He had a seizure and we're at a hospital." I could hear him trying to wake himself up. He'd landed only a few hours earlier after a long-haul flight from Europe, deciding he wanted to surprise his dad by coming home early.

I explained what happened and he tried to reassure me Stuart was a fighter and he would get through it. "I'll get there as soon as I can," he said.

When he hung up, I felt utterly alone and lost. With every beat of my heart, I could feel my distress rising. I needed someone I could lean on, but it was the middle of the night and I didn't want to ring anyone and scare them. Staring down at my phone, I realised I couldn't even remember which hospital I was in. I stepped out into the hallway trying to find a sign, but there was nothing. I panicked, bursting into tears and moaning, "I don't know where I am."

Two police officers were standing further down the corridor with someone sitting in front of them in handcuffs. One of them walked towards me. "Lady, you're at the Northern Hospital. Are you okay?" The concern of a stranger can be incredibly soothing, and he was able to calm me with just a few words. So many strangers had been similarly compassionate when I was distressed during those years, and while I may never know their names, I remember each of them for their generous spirits.

If there was one person I could ring in the middle of the night, it was my dad. At 2am I dialled his number and he answered quickly. Stumbling through the story again, I could hear his calm 'okays', and I wished he was there by my side. He was due to arrive late the next day anyway, but I begged him to come earlier. I knew he'd move heaven and earth to be with me.

As our call ended, a woman with a serious and concerned expression walked toward me. "Are you Stuart's wife?" asked the woman, and I nodded. "Yes, I am. I'm Rose."

"Rose, I'm the doctor treating your husband. He is in a critical condition. He suffered a major seizure which caused him to stop breathing." I gasped with terror at her words. "We've put him into an induced coma and attached a machine to breathe for him."

"What is wrong with him?" were the only words I could summon.

"We are not sure at this stage. We need to do further tests. He may have had a bleed on the brain, but we won't know what is going on until we get him in for a CT scan."

"If it's a bleed on the brain, isn't time of the essence? Can't you just treat him for it? Surely you can do something?"

"Unfortunately, we can't make that decision until we are sure of what happened. Due to his recent brain surgery, if it isn't a bleed and we give him those drugs, it could be fatal. The team will take him in for the scan shortly. You need to be aware of the situation because they will be wheeling him past this room and it can look quite frightening. We need to get you some support. Do you have any family here?"

"Only my daughter. She's at her boyfriend's place and I don't want to frighten her."

"Maybe some friends you can call?" I nodded. "Great, give them a call, then we'll take you in to see Stuart before he goes for the scan."

I rang many friends that night and they were all amazing. Even when the phone rang out, I would soon receive a call back, my friends knowing whatever would prompt me to reach out at such an hour was surely critical. Out-of-town friends helped me breathe through my fear, and local friends threw their clothes on and headed to the hospital to be there for me.

I needed to tell Sophie, but she was over an hour away and I didn't want her driving while she was distraught. I decided to call Zac instead. "Zac, honey, I need you to listen to me. Stuart had a seizure and is in a coma in hospital. I think Sophie needs to come here but I don't want her to drive."

"Rose, I will get her there." He was such a treasure and I knew he'd keep her calm and safe.

The doctor returned a few minutes later. "We are ready to take Stuart for the scan. You can come in now to see him." Not knowing what to expect, I nervously followed her across the corridor. She pushed open the door I had stood peering through almost an hour ago, and gestured me toward the bed where Stuart lay. There were tubes and machines everywhere, and the sounds of beeping and whirring were disorienting. Medical staff surrounded the bed ready to move him. He looked peaceful. I was too afraid to touch him, but I leant over and kissed him on the cheek.

Before I pulled away I pleaded with him, hoping he could somehow hear my voice. "Honey, please fight. Please stay strong. I need you to fight!"

They wheeled him out of the room and down the long corridor. I followed as far as I could, trying to hold myself together, but before they disappeared I called after him, "Stuart, don't leave me, please don't leave me ... I love you." Sobs racked my body and I felt someone's arms slowly wrap around me. It was the kind woman who had steered me to the waiting room earlier, and she supported me back there to wait once more.

Chapter 20
The End

Over the next few hours the waiting room filled with friends. I could feel their love, and it made such a positive difference to my energy and optimism. Sophie rushed in with Zac in her wake, falling into my arms and asking a stream of questions. "I don't know anything yet, honey, but I'm sure they will tell us when they know something."

At 7am they transferred Stuart to the intensive care unit. We were allowed in, two visitors at a time. Sophie and I walked through the cold, clinical corridors past seriously ill patients hooked up to life support, all fighting for their lives. I grabbed her hand as I felt a familiar crushing fear sweep over me. We were guided into the last room where Stuart lay motionless. There was my love, tubes running from machines into his body, being kept alive by the miracle of science. I was grateful he was alive but terrified he was in this situation. There were two nurses with him, one constantly monitoring the computer and the second checking his lines. One of them quietly explained the function of each machine and which drugs were flowing into my unconscious husband.

We stood quietly watching the screens and listening to the sounds until the doctor arrived. She revealed that Stuart was suffering from a condition which made it difficult for them to control his seizures. The next twenty-four to forty-eight hours would be crucial for assessing what damage may have been done to organs such as his brain and kidneys. I couldn't believe what I was hearing. The doctor asked a number of questions about the previous day. When I described his behavior, she told me he was most likely having absence seizures. It explained why he was ignoring me and acting strange. Realising I'd been completely oblivious to how sick he was made me feel so guilty. The doctor could see I was beating myself up.

"Rose, you weren't to know. The good thing is you woke up and got him here just in time. Focus on that. Don't look back and question yourself. You cannot change it. He is getting the best possible treatment."

"What about the antiseizure medication he's been on," I probed. "He began behaving differently after he started taking it."

"Okay, that makes sense. The drug can affect a percentage of patients in this way. We'll transition him over to another antiseizure medication with less side effects. I would like to run some tests on him now which will involve lightening the drugs. That will bring him around so we can determine if he is still experiencing seizures."

She asked for one of us to stay with Stuart so he could hear a familiar voice when he came to. Sophie volunteered immediately, so I left her there while I went to find Stuart's sons who were due shortly. I made it as far as the waiting room and was hugging a friend who had just arrived when Sophie came tearing out behind me. Her face was red and wet with tears, and she collapsed into our friend's arms. Between deep sobs she described how she had been holding Stuart's hand while the medical staff lightened his sedatives, and without warning, he suffered another traumatic seizure. She hadn't witnessed his earlier seizures and it terrified her. Now I was terrified too. If they couldn't bring him out of the coma, what would happen?

Our friend could see how distressing this was. "Let's head out to the coffee shop and get some fresh air," she suggested. I was so grateful for the way she comforted Sophie and took control. I followed them into the elevator, knowing there was no point simply standing in the corridor. As the doors opened on the lower level, I gasped. In the distance was a silhouette resembling Stuart, a man with the same build and stance who I recognized immediately as his eldest son. Sophie and I ran as fast as we could, both throwing our arms around him. I was so relieved he had made the decision to return to Australia.

The day dragged slowly while we waited for more news on Stuart, but there was no change. The doctor ceased all attempts to wake him and we were unsure what would happen next. Sophie and I eventually went home to shower and change, but quickly returned to the hospital. So many wonderful friends reached out to show their care and concern. They volunteered to pick family members up from the airport and make meals for us. The outpouring of love and support was something we will forever hold dear. It helped us through those terrifying days as Stuart teetered on the edge of that damn cliff I had come to detest.

The following day the doctor broke the bad news to us; "Stuart has developed pneumonia and his kidneys have begun to fail." They were down to 8% function and he was critical.

We held a vigil by his side – the kids, my dad, and Stuart's best mate from childhood who flew in to be with us. I asked everyone to talk to Stuart when they were with him. I wanted Stuart to hear us, hoping it would give him the strength to stay with us. I would not let anyone speak a word about him dying – it was not an option! I would do anything to keep my husband alive, and even though it didn't sound like much, I wanted everyone to shower Stuart with as much love, hope and courage as they could.

⌒⌒

Hours rolled into days and there was no change. After four days with little sleep, I decided to go home and leave the kids by Stuart's side while

I tried to rest. I fell asleep quickly, but when I woke in the early hours to an empty bed, an intense grief took hold of me. Of all the ordeals I'd faced in my life, this one crushed me. I curled up in my bed where the scent of my husband still lingered, and I wept.

Whenever I felt sad or broken, Stuart was always there to comfort me. I needed him; I needed to hear his voice. Reaching for my phone, I dialed his number. "Hi, you've called Stuart. Sorry I can't take your call but please leave a message and I'll call you back." An ache of utter longing swept through my body as Stuart's voice filled the room, and I hit redial over and over and over …

I wondered if this was how grieving widows felt. Nostalgic memories flooded my mind, but their visit was bittersweet. I could feel hope fading, but my alarm intruded, reminding me there was more yet be done. I was torn between my desire to return to Stuart's side and an urge to give in to my sorrow and hide from the world forever. I dragged myself out of bed and into the shower, briefly glimpsing the dejected woman in the mirror. I turned away from her gaze. I didn't have the strength to face her yet.

The phone rang as I wrapped a towel around my wet body. "Rose, your husband is awake." Suddenly my dull mind was alert, my heart racing. I flew on pure adrenaline, dressing quickly then catching all the green lights to the hospital. I burst through the doors and sprinted to the intensive care unit. I was elated, but anxious questions buzzed through my mind: *Was there any lasting damage from everything he'd been through? How well will he recover? Will he still be the man I married?*

I was taken straight to his side. As soon as I saw his open eyes, all my fears faded. He was fatigued and unable to focus, but he was alive and that was enough. I wrapped my arms around him and whispered, "I love you and I'm going to take you home, I promise."

Over the next few days the doctor ran tests, refusing to give us a prognosis until she finished. "You must be patient, Rose," she warned, not realising how tormenting that simple request was for someone like me. Sophie spent hours by Stuart's side, holding his hand and speaking soothingly to him. It was a strange reversal of roles, but I like to think she was returning the unconditional love Stuart had bestowed on her.

Stuart was quite unwell and still not himself. After a few days the doctor told us he would improve a little, but the trauma to his brain meant he would never work or drive again. With her words hanging heavy in the air, Stuart yelled, "How dare you tell me that. You can't stand there and tell me what I will and won't do. You don't even know me. Don't you dare give me a life sentence!"

I was shaken by Stuart's rage, but in that moment I knew the doctor's prediction was wrong. I'd just seen the only proof I needed. My husband, the stubborn and determined man who always knew everything would be okay, was still inside his broken body. All I needed to do was help him put the pieces back together.

When he left hospital he was weak and unable to get out of bed without help. The man I'd leaned on through the hardest of times, the man who showed Sophie how to believe in herself again, was now dependent on us. I quit my job, wanting to dedicate myself totally to his care, and a few months later we decided to move back to the city where we had met and married; a place where he felt inspired to recover his health. It was difficult to move away from Sophie, but she was on her own road to recovery and ready to spread her wings.

Stuart slowly improved. His determination to recover and prove the doctors wrong didn't surprise me. As I told him regularly: "Honey, you've got this."

He returned slowly to his beloved gym workouts, pushing hard through the pain to build his strength and get back to a level of health and fitness others would envy. The fog in his mind gradually lifted, and one afternoon he walked through the door with a huge smile on his face. "Guess what. I got the job!"

One Year Later

The cliff rising above the beach where Stuart and I were married is rugged and wild. The ocean stretches in an endless ribbon of blue from the jumble of rocks at the bottom of the cliff to the faint line marking the horizon. Standing high on the edge with a sea breeze whipping my hair, I thought of the many times Stuart's soothing voice had conjured this place in my mind. It was his way of calming me. Standing here now, I felt the same calmness gently wash over me.

My mind was light, wandering freely as if carried by the breeze. Memories from some of my most challenging days visited me briefly, but it was my recollections of the most loving moments that held my attention. I felt a smile touch my lips as I recalled the time Sophie whispered, "Three squeezes, Mum," after I'd brought her a home-cooked meal in the clinic. I chuckled softly as I remembered the day when Stuart and Sophie burst in to show me his tattoos while I was taking a shower. "Both you girls are stuck with me now," he'd said, and my eyes stung with tears at the sureness of his statement.

I heard the soft whisper of my name drift past on the breeze. It brought me back to the present. The salty air filled my lungs and the sun caressed my skin. Reflection is important but I don't want to live in the past. So I turned away from the cliff and looked toward the small group of people gathered behind me. Laughter rang like a sweet melody and I moved towards them, my family, the loves of my life.

Epilogue

I couldn't begin my journey of healing while my daughter and my husband were in jeopardy. I know the saying 'fit your own mask first', but love doesn't work that way. Putting the needs of those I loved before my own was an urge beyond my control, and no one could have convinced me to do otherwise. Then one day I realised no one needed me.

Stuart loved his job and was back in the role as my ever-present rock. Sophie pursued her passion for holistic health and fulfilled her childhood dream of spending her days helping people heal. By combining her new skills with her hard-won appreciation of the way trauma can lay buried within the body, she was helping others face their own life challenges.

It should have been a time of relief and joy, and I waited each day for the heaviness to lift, but my mind remained consumed by the events of the past, agonising over whether they would resurface and steal my family's future. I went back to work, but there was no spark. I knew the signs; now *I* was standing on the edge of a cliff. It was my time to heal.

On the day I met my new therapist I warned her, "You must call bullshit on me." I had become too practiced at avoiding the hardest parts of my story and I didn't want to run from it anymore. I wanted her to take me wherever I needed to go. I didn't want to stay silent. I didn't want to keep the secrets that burned like hot coals in my heart. She guided me through the layers of trauma that had been suffocating my soul, and she helped me confront the pain and the shame, the loss and the guilt, the doubt and the anxiety. They say the truth will set you free, and I was finally able to peel back the lifetime of layers obscuring my truth. Buried there, I found the sensitive and spirited girl I was before. Despite all life had thrown at her, she was still perfect and she no longer wanted to hide from the world.

~

I settled into the comfy chair across from my therapist, warming my hands on the mug of lemon and ginger tea she always offered me before we dived deep into the events of my life. But this was our last session and she had one final question for me. "Rose, do you know how diamonds are formed?"

I screwed up my face as I cast my mind back to those distant high school chemistry classes. "Is it when carbon is put under extreme pressure? It turns into diamonds."

"That's right. You've encountered intense pressure in your life, but it has transformed you into a magnificent diamond. By facing your trauma, you stopped it from tearing you apart. Instead, you're stronger, more radiant and perfectly unique."

That's the woman I am now. I didn't only survive life's tests, I found a way to emerge from them stronger and brighter.

~

The Beginning

References

* Source: Black Dog Institute
https://www.blackdoginstitute.org.au/resources-support/
suicide-self-harm/facts-about-suicide-in-australia/

** Source: 2018 ABS Recorded Crime Data, Australian Institute of
Health & Welfare, 2019a

Acknowledgements

My daughter

You are an incredible woman. You not only light up my life, but also this world. My heart beats for you.

My husband

Each step in my life led me to you, and that makes even the toughest times worthwhile. My heart beats with you.

My dad

You are my first love and the most influential man in my life. Thank you for instilling your values, passing on your determination and showing me how to find strength and courage. My heart beats because of you.

My team

The Meg Heart team helped me dig deep and find the right words to tell this story. You let my truth be heard and brought my story into the light. My heart beats stronger beside you.

My family and friends

You are not named, but you are loved. I am grateful for your support during the toughest times, for friendships that stood the test of time, and for family, who are part of me beyond time. Our hearts beat together.

About the Author

Rose cannot speak out under her real name due to laws that forbid the public disclosure of certain information in her story. She faced three choices: stay silent; tell a lesser story; or share the raw and real events from her life in a new way. That's when she found Meg Heart.

Meg Heart is a pseudonym. She is a voice for those who are silenced. The team at Meg Heart believe in the power of real stories to change the world. They support authors and storytellers who want to break their silence and protect their identity.

Important stories often go untold. People like Rose are silenced by laws. Others wish to protect the privacy of the ones they love. Some cannot bear the pressure and judgement of public life. For many, an echo of their own fear, doubt or shame silences them. Meg Heart creates a safe space for their stories to be told. Her voice speaks for them.

Powerful stories about real events wake us up and ignite a conversation. They spur us on to create a better society. They might reveal our worst, but they inspire us to become our best. Silence imprisons. Truth sets us free.

⌒

Carbon Under Pressure is the first book brought to life by Meg Heart for an author who would otherwise remain silent.

Rose lives in anonymity, but she remains committed to the promise she made in this book: to do whatever she can to curb the epidemic of youth suicide raging through our community. She hopes *Carbon Under Pressure* will start a conversation about how we can do better.

More at www.megheart.com

Printed in Australia
AUHW020904111121
355160AU00005B/15